THE THINK FACTORY

THE THINK FACTORY

∞

Managing Today's Most Precious Resource, People!

SUSAN D. CONWAY

John Wiley & Sons, Inc.

Library of Congress Cataloging-in-Publication Data:

Conway, Susan, 1947-

The think factory: managing today's most precious resource, people! / Susan Conway.

p. cm.

Includes index.

ISBN-13: 978-0-470-05519-9 (cloth)

1. Knowledge management. 2. Productivity accounting. 3. Quality assurance. I. Title.

HD30.2.C6549 2007

658.4'038—dc22

2006029328

Printed in the United States of America

10   9   8   7   6   5   4   3   2

To my grandchildren, Zachary, Isabelle, Vivien and Asher, to whom the future belongs.

Contents

Foreword

People truly are the most valuable asset in any organization—be it a company, a sports team or a government agency. How many times have you heard that a company is only as good as its people? Yet, how many companies really understand that to grow and win in the marketplace success lies in enabling its people to be the best they can be, to realize their own personal potential and maximize their contribution to the success of the company they work for?

To realize the power of the employee many different factors have to come together—work environment, tools and training. The organization needs to be ready to enable people to achieve more and realize their own potential and that of the company they work for.

When electronic mail was introduced to the business community, many people saw it as another form of communications on top of other communications options such as meetings, telephone, or physical mail. Some saw it as an attempt to turn managers into typists and something that would be utilized by only a few people. Today it would be hard to imagine any business leader who would not support the idea that electric mail use throughout the organization is critical to their success. It has allowed companies to operate 24 hours a day, 7 days a week around the world, and it has enabled collaboration, communication, and coordination among company employees, suppliers, partners, and customers. Organizations excel when they empower their people to drive the business forward. When a new technology is introduced, we may not know what the potential payoff from it will be, but history suggests we will probably underestimate its final payoff. In fact, Alan Greenspan, the former chairman of the Federal Reserve, indicated that there is no doubt that technology played a key role in the productivity gains of American business in the 1990s that positioned our economy to better deal with the inevitable ups and downs of worldwide competition.

Where competition is intense, products and services *can* become commodities overnight. The only competitive advantage is superior capability. The effective and efficient interaction among people (customers, employees, vendors), enabled by superior business procedures and technology, creates and sustains the competitive advantage. It is at this intersection that productivity resides in the Information Age.

It is the quality, not necessarily the quantity, of interactions that has become the driver of business value. We know that information technology alone cannot produce productivity benefits. We simply cannot ignore the contribution of the human side of the equation. It is not a debate but a fact that technology investments must be combined with business innovation to produce productivity improvement.

In *The Think Factory*, we come to understand the kind of business innovation that has driven productivity in the last two decades and what will shape the next wave of productivity improvement. Using the industrial factory model, technologists have, in the past, improved productivity by implementing enterprise applications that imposed tightly coupled business processes within an enterprise. These top-down projects were generally effective in producing one-time efficiency gains through standardization of information in enterprise databases, forcing processes to change, and reducing the number of people through the automation of information processing. The gains in the U.S. economy from this approach were impressive—9 percent annual productivity improvement in the final hours of the twentieth century.

Attempting to repeat the successes of the past has limited potential. What companies need is not one-time business innovation but fundamental change in their approach to business process improvement. The creation, management, and distribution of information continue to change the economic landscape. A major portion of the new economic competitiveness and productivity is being driven by changes in how information flows through, around, and to individuals within virtual organizations. Business value is created when people *use* their knowledge to inform others and facilitate the making of decisions.

The fundamental question remains: How do you measure productivity in such an environment?

If you produce widgets, the question is relatively simple to answer: widgets per hour divided by the cost of production. But if you are providing analysis services or sales proposals, how do you measure productivity? Just more is not enough. The analysis models or proposals must lead to increased sales volume. How do you determine if the models or proposals are truly improving the sales picture?

When we look at information work, we find ourselves describing how intangibles such as collaboration, search, or business intelligence applications, interact to create tangible value. Susan Conway leads us toward an understanding of what makes the think factory work. One of the key challenges has been how to define an appropriate context within which to begin the discussion. Information, people, and technology are entwined in, and integral to, almost all work efforts. The second challenge addressed in this book focuses on the definition of work in terms that can be accepted by the academic, government, and private sectors. The intent of *The Think Factory* is to establish a common basis of understanding that will guide enterprises in measuring their own ecosystems.

The methods described in the book are not theoretical but have been used successfully to improve the understanding and measurement of productivity improvements by leaders in the public and private sector.

Microsoft's own chairman and cofounder Bill Gates focused on this key issue in a memo he prepared for the Microsoft CEO Summit in May of 2006. He could not have done a better job of outlining the objective for this book when he said:

There is still a long way to travel between today's practices and a mature discipline of information work productivity. Understanding The Think Factory *is a significant step along the way.*

Robert McDowell, August 15, 2006
Vice President, Information Work
Microsoft Corporation

Acknowledgments

In developing the concepts and structuring the framework that is central to this book, I have been honored with the contributions of many brilliant and talented people within Microsoft, the academic community and associates throughout the business community. Building a framework to measure information work productivity over the past four years has found enthusiastic support with Microsoft senior leadership from Jeff Raikes, (President, MS Business Division), who extended his personal sponsorship, funding and voice to the Information Work Productivity Council (IWPC), to Steve Ballmer (Microsoft CEO), who's office co-funded the building of a working Productivity Impact Framework with the U.S. Air Force. In addition, I have benefited from the advice and council of many in the academic community including Professor Baruch Lev, New York University Stern School, Professor Dale Jorgenson, Harvard University, Professor Hal Varian, University of California, Berkeley and Professor Erik Brynjolfsson, MIT Sloan School of Management. A very special note of thanks goes to Professor Vish Krishnan, formerly of University of Texas, Austin now teaching at the University of California, San Diego. Prof. Krishnan, along with his associate, Professor Indranil Bardhan at the University of Texas, Dallas, guided the initial information work productivity studies of the IWPC in 2003-2004. The insights this combined team developed served as the foundation for the work I am privileged to share with you in this book.

I am deeply indebted to a large group of colleagues inside Microsoft and in the larger business community for their personal contributions and insights over the past four years in building the details of the program outlined here. Among the many contributors spread around the world, I would like to give special mention to Donald Koscheka and Dinesh Kumar for providing their support, brilliant ideas, creative contributions and passion for the evolution of the business value program at Microsoft. Among my colleague on the U.S. Air Force project, Susan Lau of Microsoft Consulting Services, deserves a separate mention not only for her attention to detail on the project plan, editing and assistance with the data collection but for many of excellent program diagrams you will see in Chapter 5 that depict the workflow at each step of the process. The Productivity Impact Framework (PIF) was an idea that evolved over time but would not have so quickly leaped out of the realm of research into practice if it had not been for the leadership of John Gilligan, former CIO of the U.S. Air Force, and the joint team lead by Mr. Ken Heitkamp, Ms. Hope McMahon and Lt Col Charles Dunn, for the U.S. Air Force, and Mr. John Brewer, leading the Microsoft Consulting Services team.

I am very grateful for the hours of time and thought leadership contributed by many of my business associates and customers. Leaders including Renee James, Steve Santamaria and Chuck House from Intel Corporation, Tom Davenport, Jeannie Harris and Peter Cheese at Accenture, Mohsen Moasami, Felicia Brych and Phyllis Hootman at Cisco Systems, Peter Graf and Craig Crider from SAP, Franc Gentili and Sudhir Desai from HP, James Firestone and Dan Holtshouse from Xerox Corporation. I owe a special thanks to Steve Stone, former General

Manager at Microsoft for his support throughout the research project and to Robert McDowell, Vice President at Microsoft for his advice and council over the years. This virtual team not only helped to fund the early research but also contributed of their time and energy to fuel the efforts that ultimately created a working model of information work productivity. Conceptual frameworks and research models are excellent but they require testing at the ground level to be useful. There are always leaders in the business community who seize the opportunity to contribute to the greater understanding while deepening the knowledge base within their own organizations. I owe a note of thanks to leaders such as Bob Anderson at Best Buy and S.M. Lee, Vice President of Korean Air for challenging me to use the early versions of PIF to help them measure the impact of technology improvements within their organizations. We also owe a debt of gratitude to business leaders at Intel Corporation, Cisco Systems, Pfizer, Korean Air, National City Corporation, the U.S. Air Force and numerous other businesses who have contributed data and feedback over the past five years on information work productivity.

I owe a special thank you to my editor Tim Burgard at John Wiley & Sons, who provided a steady helping hand through the development of this work and provided his editorial judgment throughout the process. Also to the John Wiley & Sons publishing team for their joint efforts in bringing all our work to a finished state.

Finally, I would like to thank my family for their five years of encouragement, support and patience during all stages of my work on the Productivity Impact Framework. If you benefit from *The Think Factory,* I would ask you to join me in thanking my husband, Jack, not only for his patience while I compiled and wrote this book but also for his diligent reviews and careful reading of each chapter.

There is a long road between theory and practice especially when trekking over new ground. I will look forward to seeing your name on the growing list of contributors to The Think Factory in the coming months and years. Join our discussion at www.productivityimpact.com/ TheThinkFactory. I will continue to post interesting case studies, respond to your questions and build new ideas with you as we journey deeper into the 21st century.

Susan Conway

August 2006

Part One

CLARIFYING THE INSIDE-OUT WORKPLACE

The twentieth century witnessed the industrial revolution. The perfection of its iconic symbol, the assembly-line factory, brought changes not only to the way businesses run but to the very fabric of the society at large. The evolution continues into the twenty-first century, where businesses are becoming cubicle-lined think factories. The essence of work has moved from the production of consumable, tangible commodities to the production of concepts, information, processes, and services. Innovation—the ability to turn knowledge into value-producing assets—is the new golden key to business success. Finding the delicate balance between streamlined production and the innovation-friendly environment will be the foundation of productivity in the coming decades. A fundamental change has occurred in the nature and role of information in business.

The enablement of the information worker (I-worker) and consistency of information flow will ignite the next wave of business productivity.

Information, like rainwater falling to the earth, permeates the entire enterprise. It enters the system and seeps into every nook and cranny. As it moves from one I-worker to another, it undergoes the processes of change, renewal, and creation. Just as the rainwater changes color and viscosity as it passes through the layers of rock and dirt in the earth, information is modified, combined, and re-formed as it is used, acted on, and reacted to by the people, processes, and infrastructure of the enterprise. Just as water finds resistance in the form of rocks and debris that cause partial or temporary dams, information can become constrained or locked within the organization by a variety of barriers or can even seep out the edges and seams of the enterprise. Barriers may be as simple as a backlog of manual data or as complicated as incompatible technologies. Information streams can also become diverted by people hording or lacking the skills, technology, or desire to collaborate. Finding a way to improve and secure the information flow through clarification and facilitation of the stream is the first objective in the journey to achieving increased information work (I-work) productivity.

I-work productivity starts with the optimization of the flow of information through the organization. Just as water is the lifeblood of the earth, information is the life-giving force of the enterprise. As rainwater brings life to the dry earth, information creates wealth in information-centric organizations. Stop the flow of water and the grass dries up; not enough snowpack and the trees do not bloom in the spring, causing the life cycle to end. The same is true of the information flow within the enterprise.

Throughout this book, we will refine the concepts of I-work and I-workers as well as the critical success factors required to foster productivity in the new think factories. At this point, you could be asking yourself: Are "I-work" and "I-worker" just other names for "knowledge" and "knowledge worker," as defined in 1959 by Peter Drucker?[1] Although there are parallels between the terms, I-work goes well beyond Drucker's notion of knowledge-based work. Over the past 40 years, the term "knowledge work" has taken on competing definitions, and along the way misperceptions have developed about what it actually means from both an individual and an organizational standpoint. Furthermore, a survey of the most common definitions of the term "knowledge workers" results in an image that is not inclusive enough of the I-worker roles in most organizations today and excludes large segments of the information-bound workforce.

Defining information versus knowledge work is often a matter of insight and point of view. Consider the case of a hospital chief executive: She would probably consider her doctors or nurses to be knowledge workers, but would she consider her administrative staff knowledge workers? Would the CIO of an automotive manufacturer consider factory floor supervisors to be knowledge workers? The fact that we need to stop to think about our answers raises the question of whether the term "knowledge worker" is a broad enough framework for the current marketplace to describe information-intensive workers and the role technology plays in that work. This new world of information-centric work and information-bound workers drives a change in both our approach to and perspective on productivity and even the nature of work. One of the goals of this book is to eliminate some of these challenges and provide a framework for a broader view of the information-centric workplace.

Through the definition and description of the Productivity Impact Framework (PIF), we explore the impact organizational and technology changes can have on this evolving landscape. PIF also provides a venue for discussing how to apply the baselining concepts of Lean Six Sigma (LSS) to I-work.[2] To measure, it is necessary to define the components of the process. Just as each assembly line in a factory has a purpose, each work scenario, or flow, within the I-work business has a core objective or function that can be measured. At the center of each work scenario should be a valued deliverable(s) that can be measured not only in terms of customer satisfaction but in relation to defects (rework), speed (time), and velocity (cycle time) for production. The I-work process consumes not only raw materials—information—but utilizes skilled labor to produce the required output. This invisible workflow is composed of the business procedures linked together by enabling technology that represents the assembly line within the Think Factory. The PIF approach was designed to help organizations define and measure the impact of technology on the core functionality of each business scenario. It is against this core functionality that we can measure and monitor variance while driving toward improved effectiveness and efficiency. The new think factory demands a one-stop shopping experience for information consumers. Fragmented and disjointed information points generate chaos, increase entropy, and inhibit innovation. Information retrieval and reuse should not require extensive training or specialized skills. Mapped and documented information flows not only enhance productivity but also help fulfill regulatory requirements for clarity and information transparency. We will look at evolving think factories in the commercial and public sector, learn about their experiences measuring I-work, and explore what can be done to enhance the performance of these unique environments. Just as Fredrick Taylor reinvented industrial work with task analysis, a new perspective is now required that examines the nature and flow of work throughout the enterprise and how it supports and fosters innovative information-centric work.[3]

Every change begins with a vision and a decision to take action. The change in the nature of work has generated fear not only about our local economy but about the implications for the global economic network. Economic models have been continuously revised, reflecting uncertainty and doubt.[4] A strong consensus has emerged that economic growth is tied to the global flow of information used by people and enabled by technology. In this book we will further explore the impact of information technology and labor productivity. If the drumbeat of the Industrial Age was faster, better, and cheaper products, the mantra of the Information Age is faster, more consistent and focused information.

ENDNOTES

1. Peter Drucker, *Managing in the Next Society* (2002).

2. Lean Six Sigma is essentially the quality structure driven by Six Sigma, as originated by Motorola in the 1980s, combined with the concepts of Lean Production (making work faster). LSS focuses on delivering a product/service to your customer (internal or external) with speed and quality. LSS has a strong emphasis on teamwork (collaboration) and basing improvement on data and facts (resulting from baselining/benchmarking). The collaboration and process-based aspects of LSS are some of the key ingredients that allow us to map LSS concepts to I-work.

3. Fredrick W. Taylor, *The Principles of Scientific Management* (1911).

4. As quoted in Dale Jorgenson, "Accounting for Growth in the Information Age," 2005. Congressional Budget Office (2000) on official forecasts and Economics and Statistics Administration (2000), p. 60, on private forecasts.

❦ 1 ❦

The Essence of I-Work

As the twenty-first century opened "...The world was producing between 1 and 2 exabytes of unique information per year, which is roughly 250 megabytes for every man, woman, and child on earth. An exabyte is a billion gigabytes, or 10^{18} bytes. Printed documents of all kinds comprise only .003% of the total."[1]

All this information creates noise and threatens organizational paralysis. To remedy this problem, businesses need to structure information and streamline information work (I-work) to facilitate productivity. In the last half century, technology has not only generated a vast storehouse of data, but has also caused a geometric explosion of new information and knowledge. Within many organizations, data are being recorded at unprecedented speed and granularity, often without usable structure or defined goals. By harnessing information, the lifeblood of business today, we enable people to turn data into insight, transform ideas into action, and turn change into opportunity.

DEFINING THE INVISIBLE
FACTORY SPACE

In 1959, when Peter Drucker looked at the emerging work world, he saw the revolutionary change from an industrial society to a more office-based society of people who rely on technology to perform their jobs.[2] The technology-based revolution Drucker envisioned promised to open our vision, unburden our backs, and free our minds for more productive work.

The concept of knowledge work and knowledge workers has certainly flourished since the 1950s, but, as Drucker noted in 2002, we have not yet mastered the challenge of fully defining knowledge work.[3] If we are to manage work, we need to have a measure of success. If we are to measure something, it is necessary to define it. The expanding definition of information-centric work has now exceeded Drucker's definition of highly paid scientists and professionals on one side and transaction workers (inputting data) on the other. Over the past 20 years the technology revolution has achieved a great deal of notice, drawing attention away from the more subtle changes in the workplace. The transformation that is perhaps less noticeable, but just as important, is the growing intensity of information use in nearly every type of job category—from call center representatives to truck drivers and, yes, even industrial factory workers.

The changing nature of work has brought a new tension to the workplace. The routine nature of manufacturing has given way to the mental stress of managing ever-increasing streams of complex information. The degree of information intensity follows the increase in work complexity and environmental uncertainty, as shown in Figure 1.1. As computers multiplied across workstations and desktops, the geometric increase in the amount and volume of information has increased the complexity of our work. The more routine transaction work, prevalent in the

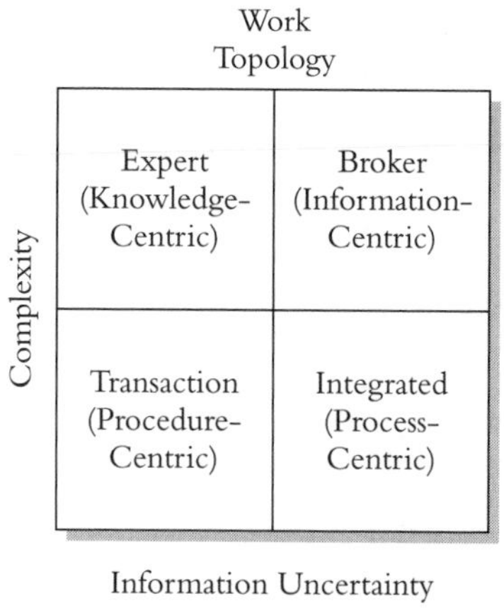

Work
Topology

FIGURE 1.1 Work Topology

early days of office computing, has been replaced by the information coordination performed by increasing numbers of managers and supervisors. The increase in work complexity brings with it the more subtle, and often more stressful, impact of information multiplication that has led to the increase in work uncertainty. Decisioning (the process of making, approving and executing decisions), along with information, is rapidly migrating across and downward through increasingly flattened organizations. It is this dual pressure, as opposed to technology, that is rapidly changing the nature of and the requirements for interconnected workplace technologies.

The wide variety of solutions and the growth of technology options over the past five years is a testament to the varied communication requirements and information processing needs of the different types of information workers (I-workers), as indicated in Figure 1.2. Business situations have different information requirements. Consider the different types of computer support required by aircraft designers and data center operators. Aircraft design requires expert I-workers who are highly independent (low uncertainty) and who are capable of highly complex work. Data

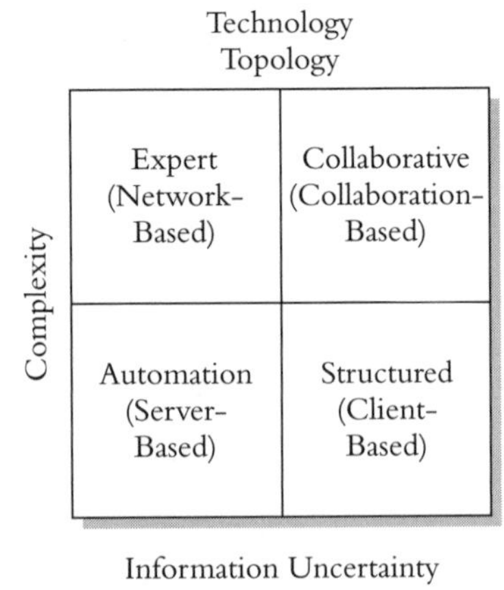
Technology
Topology
Expert
(Network-
Based)
Collaborative
(Collaboration-
Based)
Automation
(Server-
Based)
Structured
(Client-
Based)
Complexity
Information Uncertainty

FIGURE 1.2 Technology Topology

centers, with their focused workload, require less complex work. Both have work that is highly independent (low uncertainty) requiring infrequent synchronization and coordination by the players. The big difference is that aircraft design is also highly complex, requiring workers to manage information in volatile and somewhat less structured conditions. The differences in the work modes provide an insight into the changing drivers within the information-centric workplace. While office productivity and basic communication applications may suffice for the data center, or transaction work, the more complex invention/innovation work of designers is best served by network connectivity—the ability to safely store, manage, and share from common locations with minimal interrupt. Other work scenarios will have other challenges. A structured workplace, such as a service center, with an uncertain work demand but low complexity is best serviced by client-server technology. This allows for the input and update of work orders as technicians complete jobs and an end-of-day reconciliation. Finally, coordination work, of executives, managers, or salespeople, is characterized by both high complexity and high interdependence. Though all three classes of technologies may be useful here collaborative technologies are emerging to support these complex synchronous needs.[4]

The growth in information complexity and work interdependence has driven the need for more collaborative and enabling technology solutions. The better the fit between the technology and the type of I-work, the more likely the technology is to improve output.

The evolution of information-centric work has incorporated knowledge work as a subset of the much broader occupational category: *information work*. In the leading edge economies, the great majority of workers constantly use data, information, and knowledge—each to varying degrees—in their jobs. They create, manage, share, receive, and/or manipulate information. To compensate for the change in the nature of work, the U.S. Bureau of Labor Statistics (BLS) redefined and reclassified its major categories of work in 2000. The 2000 Standard Occupational Classification (SOC) System was developed in response to a growing need for a universal occupational classification system. Such a system allows government agencies and private industry to produce comparable data. Federal agencies collecting occupational data use the SOC, providing a means to compare occupational data across agencies.[5] Although this system helps in our understanding of the number and types of workers involved in I-work, we still were not able to measure the tempo, or flow, of this work.

The need to define and measure effectiveness and efficiency in the think factory became apparent in the early stages of its evolution. The continuing I-work evolution is driving a redefinition not only of the measurement of work but of the impact of work enablement. Despite a massive infusion of information technology into think factories over the past 30 years, a corresponding growth in work productivity did not seem to materialize. As MIT economist Robert Solow quipped in 1987, "You can see the computer age everywhere but in the productivity statistics."[6] Solow later wrote that it was not that he doubted that technology could contribute to productivity but rather that we still have no effective way of measuring or verifying its impact on I-work. The simple fact that the average U.S. productivity has risen over the last 50 years at twice the rate of the average hours of work would seem to indicate that the technology-based changes in the workplace have had a significant impact on our ability to cope with information-intensive work. Technology continues to flow into the workplace and businesses continue to struggle with quantifying the impact of the investment.

Productivity is a well-established economic concept, but the equations used to generate productivity numbers are tuned to industrial work. It is generally recognized that traditional productivity calculations seek to measure tangible assets, such as physical capital and labor measured by product output. This thinking still rules the majority of economic calculations. We continue to count physical products (production) and time spent (labor) as the basis of business value. Some forms of I-work still produce or move around physical assets, but often information, or knowledge itself, is the output. In such businesses, we have few means of recording and measuring the outputs, so productivity is ill defined at best.

While information technologies appear to be useful, as Solow pointed out, their productivity and quality impacts are far from clear. Call center workers can answer more customer calls with highly scripted workflow systems, but are their customers satisfied enough to buy more products? Managers certainly can know more about the activities of truck drivers or traveling salespeople with global positioning systems (GPSs), but have these advances improved productivity? Managers clearly can create more documents with their word processors and presentation tools, but what is the bottom-line impact? Even though I-workers employ many different tools in their jobs, these tools remain fragmented and can be disruptive to the workflow. No improvement comes without a cost. New concepts, products or services as well as the tools used to produce them often require an investment in training and workflow redesign.

Information by itself provides little advantage. It has been 20 years since *Megatrends*[7] author John Naisbitt warned, "We are drowning in information but starved for knowledge." As information becomes the foundation of economic wealth, the phenomenon that Naisbitt noted is rapidly becoming a legal and logistical nightmare for many companies. To benefit from information as a value-generating mechanism, businesses must adopt and apply methods that will connect I-workers across all areas of the organization so that they may put this treasure trove of information to work—without adding substantial amounts of labor. Companies with structures that align and organize information to their strategies and I-work processes will succeed in this new environment. Every service provider seems to have a solution to this paradigm, but most do not address the fundamental changes required to truly enhance and mobilize I-work.

Six types of performance measures reflect the correct balance of the impact of technology and procedure improvements on:

- Cycle time
- Cost
- Quality
- New product innovation
- On-time completion
- Customer satisfaction

Studies indicate that effectiveness clearly has a significant positive impact on all six performance measures.

Efficiency, however, has a *significant* positive impact only on the cycle time, cost, and on-time completion measures. [8]

RIGHT ANSWER, WRONG SCENARIO

To promote productivity, information-centric enterprises need to make changes to both procedures and technology in order to maximize performance and financial outcomes. Not only do these changes need to be compatible with the work; they also must resonate with the culture of the enterprise. Earlier we discussed the problems of mis-aligning technology and work, such as adding structured technology to highly volatile and complex work. The same logic holds true for organizational structures, as outlined in Figure 1.3; introducing highly collaborative technology into an automated (transaction-based) organization could actually reduce productivity (throughput). In 2004 a leading pharmaceutical firm complained that it could not get its product development teams to embrace collaborative technologies such as instant messaging (IM). The root of the

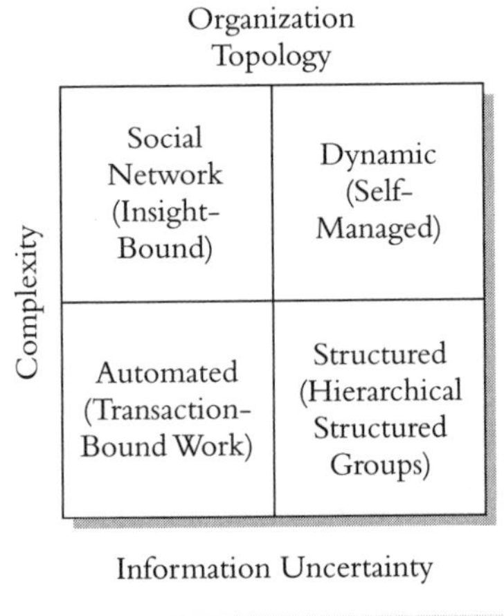

Organization
Topology

	Social Network (Insight-Bound)	Dynamic (Self-Managed)
	Automated (Transaction-Bound Work)	Structured (Hierarchical Structured Groups)

Complexity (vertical axis, left)

Information Uncertainty

FIGURE 1.3   Organizational Topology

problem was a misalignment between the (expert and bro-ker) work and a hierarchical organization structure bound by tradition and government regulations. To make the tech-nology work in this situation, the organization needed to see the necessity of changing its structure and the technol-ogists needed to meet the demands for tracking and trans-parency required by the regulatory agency. Other examples of organizational constraints are easier to visualize: In data entry centers, we can envision in our mind's eye the ineffi-ciency of people trying to hold virtual meetings on data input issues that are better handled by a simple request to the supervisor for resolution. Organizations will not realize significant performance improvements if technology is used only to improve the quantity of outputs and inputs, ignor-ing the effectiveness and quality of the outcomes.

Economists and management scientists have conducted hundreds of studies and written thousands of words attempting to provide some guidance to the business community on what might be influencing productivity in the information-centric economies. Many observers have noted the large gains made in the U.S. economy as opposed to the apparent decline in productivity in Europe and Asia. One common theme in these studies and presentations has been the extent to which the environments have embraced technology and supported workers in using that technology to change how they work. Professor Dale Jorgenson of Harvard University has summarized some of the forward thinking on what enables an information-centric environment. He states: Investment in information technology leads to the growth of productive capacity in technology-using industries. He fur-ther explains that:

❖ Average labor productivity (ALP) growth [in the United States] from 1948 to 2002 increased 2.23 percent per year while hours worked increased only 1.23 percent per year.

❖ Output growth is the sum of growth in hours and average labor pro-ductivity.

Given these facts, Jorgenson concludes:

❖ ALP depends on capital deepening—that is, appropriately placed information technology investment to underpin labor capability.

❖ 30 percent of output improvements can be attributed to improved labor quality.

❖ Labor quality is a correlation of the enablers that allow workers to produce faster, better, cheaper:

  ❖ Technology

  ❖ Training

  ❖ Procedures[9]

The fact that in 1994 the BLS released a new multifactor productivity measure adding (to hours worked) a constant quality index of labor input reinforces Jorgenson's argument on the quality of labor.

Improving I-work productivity requires measuring the degree to which enablers (procedures, technology, and training) support the speedy delivery of quality products and services. These criteria have guided the development of the Productivity Impact Framework (PIF) methodology and the associated Productivity Impact Measures (PIMs) discussed throughout the book that are meant to support the business community in assessing and improving information-centric work. Part II of this book outlines the assessment process and describes in more depth the components of I-work that can be strengthened to improve its productivity. The essential measurement goal is to deepen the quality of I-work through investments in technology, training, and/or procedural improvements. The goal is not to develop a complete business value model but rather establish the statistical signposts for a summary-level business case where improvement is needed.

REAL-WORLD EXAMPLES

Theory is wonderful but real-world examples make concepts actionable. PIF has been applied to a variety of organizations in a variety of industries, each with its own unique challenges and work scenarios. The first two cases introduced here involve the U.S. Air Force Senior Leadership Management Office (AFSLMO) team led at the time by Colonel Steven Kwast and the Korean Air team sponsored by chief information officer Mr. S. M. Lee. Both organizations have been kind enough to share their recent experiences with PIF.

 ## CASE STUDY 1: U.S. AIR FORCE SUCCESSION PLANNING (JULY 2005–JANUARY 2006)

Col Kwast's AFSLMO team was responsible for executive (Colonel) succession planning. The task Kwast had taken on was to streamline an overtaxed and operationally outdated function. The goal was to create a high-performance team able to deliver a quality service while reducing the overtime required in accomplishing the work scenarios.

The team began by taking a top-down view of the work required to meet customer needs. The AFSLMO customers included both promotion candidates and general officers seeking to fill positions around the world. The team identified three key work scenarios: game planning, contender management, and colonel action board (CAB). The Productivity Opportunity Map (POM) process, which is explained in detail later in Chapter 5, revealed potential opportunities for improvement in all three of the identified work scenarios. Three challenges crossed all functional areas:

- ❖ Data transparency
- ❖ Content sharing
- ❖ Information aggregation

Although these discoveries were not astonishing, the statistical exposure of the challenge areas validated the group's gut hunch about what they needed to fix. Group members narrowed down the procedures, activities, and technologies that were indeed challenged and that were a major contributing cause of the productivity gap. By using a focused approach and setting improvement targets, the leadership could clearly see that success would be achieved through reducing the work effort by improving collaboration and reducing rework. The group not only succeeded, achieving a 14 percent reduction in work effort, but exceeded the original target by 9 percent. As we discuss how to build an assessment program, we will review how the Air Force team designed the data collection, analyzed the results, and achieved its goals.

CASE STUDY 2: KOREAN AIR (JUNE 2005–ONGOING)

Measuring the success of enterprise-wide productivity improvements is very challenging. Lee's team at Korean Air needed to identify productivity opportunities to target for the 11,000+ headquarters and region information-centric workforce. First, using the PIF methodology, the team worked through a top-down opportunity mapping exercise. This exercise interviewed subject matter experts in eight major functional areas and established common opportunities across this diverse I-worker audience focusing on two targets:

❖ Communications
❖ Wait time for approvals

The team found sufficient potential improvement opportunities in personal (asynchronous) communications across all eight functional areas within the headquarters organization. It also discovered strong indicators of challenges in the approval time throughout the same organization. One unit was chosen as a vertical study to highlight these challenges as part of the baseline assessment. When the baseline assessment was completed, the team was able to narrow the improvement target to four focal areas:

- ❖ Reduce the data transfer latency (elapse time) encountered when requesting information (content management).
- ❖ Expend less effort to update documents (content sharing).
- ❖ Improve person-to-person information delays (collaboration).
- ❖ Expend less effort to receive approvals (communications).

The executive steering committee now felt it was able to make a rational business decision about technology upgrades, procedure changes, and plan training to improve enterprise productivity. The gains recommended were a modest 3 percent measured at the functional unit level. However, a gain of 3 percent across an organization of this size is a considerable savings in terms of process cycle efficiency. Beyond the obvious labor cost is the potential improvement in customer satisfaction resulting from faster, higher-quality delivery of services in a very competitive and financially challenged industry.

Throughout our discussion of building and analyzing productivity impact studies, we will make reference to both case studies.

As we saw in the Korean Air case study, improvement estimates on enterprise-wide projects can be difficult to rationalize from the top down. Looking at the potential of such a project from the individual up gives us some perspective. Many enterprises have recently launched productivity projects aimed at gaining back at least 8 to 16 hours a month for each employee. The theory is that people will have time to put quality into the work they do, accomplish more while reducing overtime, and generally become more satisfied with their jobs. Keeping such goals in mind, we try to analyze the impact of changes to individual behaviors on the larger enterprise. In the Korean Air study, we asked questions such as What is the potential result of an organization reducing the total average number of meetings by one per week (returning one hour of work per week per employee)? Based on the average hourly cost of labor, the enterprise has the potential of improving its bottom line by $56,000 in recovered time. If we add employee time in these meetings, the firm might recover an additional $300,000 to $500,000 (taking into account the additional time spent on managing information now received at the desktop). While substantial, the real savings for Korean Air is not in the minutes saved per day per employee but in the overall improvement of process cycle efficiency and through people achieving higher-quality output through better utilization of information and technology. Based on these and other similar analytics, Korean Air leaders chose an improvement project that included changes in communications (messaging and collaboration) and content-sharing (content management) technology and related procedures. Since the improvement cycle for such a large project is long—one year in this case—the results are not yet in. We are looking forward to benchmarking their success in the coming months.

These case studies and other examples discussed in later chapters provide a way to visualize the impact of PIF on an organization at both the enterprise and the functional level.

CONCLUSION

The Solow Paradox—we see computers everywhere but in the productivity statistics—has been displaced by the economics of the Information Age. Just as the assembly line changed the twentieth century's industrial landscape, information technology has indelibly changed, and will continue to change, the economic landscape of the twenty-first century. Business investment strategies must be balanced between technology acquisition and the deepening of labor capital. Deepening the capability and ability of the work force allows managers to, as Fredrick Taylor[10] noted nearly 100 years ago, find the right challenge for each person, provide the guidance and means of production, and pay well for increased output. Deepening the investment in people and procedures to capture the advantage offered by technology is the key to economic success in the coming decade. Restructuring the work environment to facilitate the flow of information opens the door not only to productivity gains but to the information transparency required by recent regulatory rules relating to corporate governance.

ENDNOTES

1. Hal Varian, "How Much Information?" University of California at Berkeley, www.sims.berkeley.edu/research/projects/how-much-info/summary.html.

2. Drucker, Peter, *Landmarks of Tomorrow*, Transaction Publishers, New Edition, 1996.

3. Peter Drucker, "Managing in the Next Society," St. Martin Press, NY, 2002.

4. Vish Krishnan and Indranil Bardhan, "The Impact of Information Technology on Information Work," Information Work Productivity Council (IWPC) Annual Research Report, September 27, 2004.

5. The SOC is designed to cover all occupations in which work is performed for pay or profit, reflecting the current occupational structure in the United States. The 2000 SOC is the result of a cooperative effort of all the U.S. federal agencies that use the occupational classification system to maximize the usefulness of occupational information collected by the U.S. Federal Government.

   All occupations are clustered into one of 23 major groups. Within these major groups are 96 minor groups, 449 broad occupations, and 821 detailed occupations. Occupations with similar skills or work activities are grouped at each of the four levels of hierarchy to facilitate comparisons. For example, "Life, Physical and Social Science Occupations" (19-0000) is divided into four minor groups,

"Life Scientists" (19-1000), "Physical Scientists" (19-2000), "Social Scientists and Related Workers" (19-3000), and "Life, Physical and Social Science Technicians" (19-4000). "Life Scientists" contains broad occupations, such as "Agriculture and Food Scientists" (19-1010) and "Biological Scientists" (19-1020). The broad occupation "Biological Scientists" includes detailed occupations such as "Biochemists and Biophysicists" (19-1021) and "Microbiologists" (19-1022).

6. Robert McGuckin and Kevin Stiroh, "Computers Can Accelerate Productivity Growth," *Issues in Science and Technology* (Summer 2000).

7. Naisbitt, John, Megatrends, Wagner Books, NY, 1984.

8. Krishnan, ibid.

9. Dale Jorgenson, "Accounting for Growth in the Information Age," Harvard University (2005).

10. Frederick W. Taylor, in 1911, published his principle work, The Principles of Scientific Management. This work outlined the application of scientific methods to the management of labor. Scientific management calls for the optimizing of the tasks workers perform and simplifying the jobs enough so that workers can be trained to perform their individual tasks in a sequence of motions that quickly and efficiently complete the work required. Prior to scientific management, work was taught through the apprenticeship programs—where workers learned the 'appropriate' method of completing their tasks.

❧ 2 ❧

Cubicle-Lined Factory

In the Information Age, unlike previous eras, the foundation for wealth—information—can be found everywhere. Generating value in such an environment is the ability to organize and apply that information in more productive and channeled manners. It is the unique understanding of the essence of information generation and information work (I-work) and how it allows individuals and organizations to drive productivity and profitability.

The spotlight that has focused on knowledge workers for the past 30 or so years is expanding to illuminate other workers who make intensive use of information in their jobs. In the United States and other advanced economies, this is a large and growing portion of the overall workforce.

Based on data from the U.S. Bureau of Labor Statistics (BLS) (see Figure 2.1), we can estimate that nearly 88 percent of the 142 million nonfarm workforce employees in the United States were engaged in some form of I-work by the turn of the twenty-first century. A quick summary of the 2003 BLS statistics shows that there are roughly 124 million information workers (I-workers in the country. We need to learn more about how these I-workers can do their work more productively. Any broad-based improvements to I-work could bring substantial benefits to the economy and society.

One way of looking at the value of I-work is seeing it as a product produced through informed action and knowledge-based collaboration. Informed action is I-work performed by people acting directly on the information delivered to them: They act or react to this information. Knowledge-based collaboration involves the creation, transformation, or transmission of information in and around the decision-making and creative processes. This distinction is important in order to understand the concept of I-work (directly acting on or reacting to information). In order to produce value, information must either be acted upon (I-work) or used to conduct business (knowledge-based collaboration). Just as information is not useful unless it is acted upon, knowledge gains business value only when it is used in the development of products/services, the fulfillment of customer demands, the generation of customer demand, and/or the planning and management of the enterprise. In order, then, to understand I-work, we need to break it down into business processes and activities involving either informed action or knowledge-based collaboration. Productivity can be measured and improved only at the point within the workflow where information is transformed or acted upon.

FIGURE 2.1 Information Worker Labor Statistics

The Bureau of Labor Statistics has defined 21 major occupational groups to provide an understanding of the U.S. workforce. There is also significant data on how U.S. workers use technology as part of their occupation (see Dept of Labor O★NET for occupational job details). As part of work done by the Information Work Productivity Council in 2003, the following taxonomy was applied to this data:

★ All U.S. Workers: All nonfarm employees, including self-employed in the United States based on BLS for February 2006.

★ Information Workers: Number of people (according to BLS associated categories) that would fit the definition of I-worker — approximately 88% of the total U.S. nonfarm workforce.

This analysis was done for the U.S. market, but the segmentation would probably be very similar for most developed markets.

Population	Estimate
Total nonfarm U.S. workforce	141,994,000
Total I-Worker U.S. workforce★	121,175,000
Office based	69,574,000
Other	54,601,000

★ Worker categories associated with office and related (floor) work including managers, services, sales and production occupations.

Source for statistics: http://stats.bls.gov/news.release/empsit.t10.htm

WORKING IN THE INFORMATION WORLD

Measuring the think factory requires a correlation of multiple variables to identify the improvement opportunities within a target work scenario. Building this image requires not only identifying the players (roles) and their place in the overall organization (navigation) but the activities (behaviors) that are expected, the technology (enablers) used, and the deliverables (output) to be produced. (See Figure 2.2.)

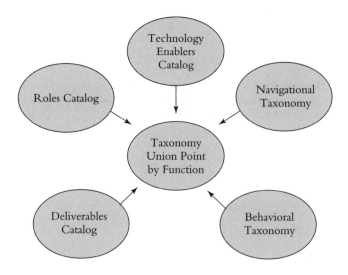

FIGURE 2.2   Five Taxonomy Structure

It is at the intersection of these five taxonomies that we can measure efficiency and effectiveness (E/E). Most of us understand business initiatives around efficiency: Do it faster and cheaper. The two greatest expenses in the I-work space are:

1. *Labor* expended in using information and the labor cost of generating and managing knowledge
2. *Technology,* including the infrastructure, to support the distribution of information

Effectiveness—doing it better—is more complex and harder to quantify. Over the course of the past two decades, the drumbeat of quality has been heard in every sector of the economy. Doing work faster, resulting in less expense, should not result in poor quality being delivered to the customer. It is important not only to view the efficiency aspects of use/utilization; as with any assembly line, the appropriate alignment of the work is essential to optimization.

THE WORK WE DO: ROLES AND TECHNOLOGY

Although all value-generating I-work involves informed action or knowledge-based collaboration, not all I-workers fall neatly into one group. Experts often not only create information (from knowledge) but also are required to transmit that information to others. This point is important to remember as we discuss the nature of I-work: Although the majority of our work might neatly fall into one category or another, we all perform work across then entire spectrum of I-work. Productivity is improved by examining the primary function for a role and seeing that the enablers are properly aligned to that function.

With any initiative to improve I-worker productivity, it is important to begin by understanding the work in terms of the basic activities expected and behaviors required. In Figure 2.3, I-work has been divided into four segments. Looking from the right top in a clockwise fashion, the work activities indicate that Collaborators and Experts work primarily with knowledge to support decision making. Working on the creation and transmission of knowledge often dictates desktop technology and extensive connectivity for research and collaboration. Transactors and Integrators, in contrast, are heavy users of information in their job tasks or actions. They spend more of their time utilizing, rather than producing, information content. Although the enablement decision is very dependent on the industry and specific environment, asynchronous communications technologies and mobile synchronous devices are often the key to enabling the utilization of information for these I-workers.

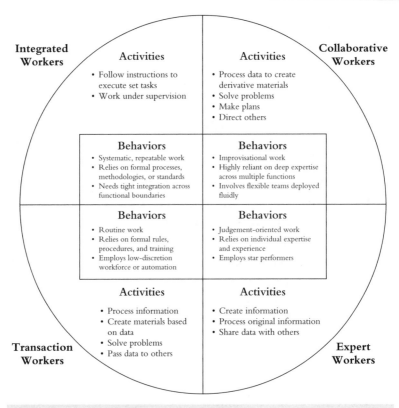

FIGURE 2.3 Aligning Work and Behaviors

Looking at the work behaviors, we divide the matrix horizontally and note that primarily autonomous individuals do transaction and expert work whereas Integrators and Collaborators tend to work collaboratively. The degree to which collaboration is required strongly influences the type of technology, environment, and connectivity required for the role.

Understanding the required activities and expected behaviors is critical to aligning the supporting technology and streamlining the work procedures. As with operations in manufacturing, we need to identify and associate the work modes (activities and behaviors) with the specific work scenarios to improve productivity.

Same Work, Different Function

Measuring five key, or common, I-work behaviors provides us with an image of the work activities and a basis for measuring output. The five behaviors include:

- Content generation and management
- Personal communication (asynchronous)
- Collaboration or teamwork (synchronous communication)
- Problem solving and analysis
- Search and retrieval (research)

By aligning the types of work with the people doing the work, we create a more holistic image of the transaction. Building the initial alignment model requires a comparative analysis of the components. To help understand the alignment of I-work and the I-work roles, the Information Work Productivity Council (IWPC) funded a series of studies.[1] The Council took its lead from Tom Peters's statement that "in the new economy, all work is project work."[2] The studies focused on project management as the work scenario and the project manager as the I-worker.[3] The trends in project work have shown us that the balance of work in leading edge information-centric organizations will continue to shift from production (content generation and asynchronous communication) to plan/design work (collaboration and search/retrieve). This shift in emphasis is noted in the increase in collaboration and analysis work for coordination roles such as those seen in Case Study 1, the U.S. Air Force succession planning team, where the majority of the roles were coordination. This shift has been enabled by improved practices that rely on advances in technologies. Recent Productivity Impact Framework (PIF) studies with public agencies and private companies show that work groups encounter productivity challenges when performance support lags behind changes in work modes. In the next few pages we will use the PIF alignment model to see how PIF views each role and the potential impact technology and procedure changes can have on those roles.

Envisioning I-Work

Like the roles of the I-worker, I-work has a somewhat set pattern. As shown in Figure 2.4, when PIF looks at I-work, the analysis examines five types of work, or behaviors: content generation and management, personal or asynchronous communications, collaboration or synchronous communications, problem solving and analysis and search and retrieve or research.

Content generation and management, personal communication, and research are fundamentally individual work behaviors or activities that are performed by individuals with limited or no team interaction. Content generation in this context is the individual work effort to construct and form content or post content for others to work on. Group participation in content formation becomes a form of collaboration. Communication is often thought of as an interactive behavior or activity. Personal, or asynchronous, communication is associated as an individual work behavior since it involves essentially one-way or potentially limited forms of interaction such as telephone (involving an individual talking with one other person or leaving voice mail), e-mail (but not instant messaging that provides a form of interaction) or outgoing memos or mail. Research, the searching for and retrieving of information, is the third I-work behavior that is almost exclusively associated with an individual (non-collaborative) work mode.

Collaboration, or synchronous I-work, is, of course, a team activity, as is content sharing. Content creation, within enterprises, is often not only a team effort but often a virtual engagement sometimes spanning time zones, cultures and organizations. Problem solving and analysis are very often, but not exclusively, collaborative in nature. All four I-work roles engage in all five types of I-work behaviors. It is the degree of participation, or use of the behavior that distinguishes one role from another. We all attend meetings, but the degree to which collaborative events dominates the work day determines the role type. The models and personas developed next illustrate how these work behaviors are utilized by each of the four I-worker roles.

Figure 2.4 Five Basic I-Work Behaviors

Experts

Experts are those workers who most often perform independently, with little to no supervision, to create and apply high-value forms of information or knowledge to their work. While they may also interact with others in making decisions, as collaborators do, or analyze data, as transactors do, their role is largely that of a subject matter expert or solo professional practitioner. Some physicians, lawyers, and consultants are primarily in this category of I-worker. The expert worker model we use for our productivity impact studies shows that these types of workers spending nearly half of their work efforts focused on analysis and content generation. (See Figure 2.5.)

 EXPERT I-WORKER PERSONA

Mary is an attorney specializing in employment law. She spends most of her time doing legal research, mostly using online sources, creating documents, solving problems, and analyzing data. She is a mobile worker, depending on her laptop, cell phone, and PDA to keep on schedule and in contact. Although she keeps in touch with her paralegal, she performs most of her tasks independently.

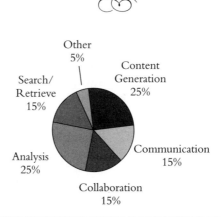

FIGURE 2.5   I–Work Distribution: Experts

Transaction Workers

Workers in the transaction segment, such as data analysts and financial clerks, make some independent decisions and might build upon existing information to generate new information, but are mostly supported by information or instructions from other people. The I-Work distribution model clearly demonstrates that transaction workers spend nearly double the time in content generation than expert workers but much less time searching and analyzing. (See Figure 2.6.)

Transaction-based I-workers may also interpret the information presented to them and process, or channel, it into other forms for reuse. If we again look at the model for transaction workers, we find that the majority of their work effort is focused on content generation—manipulating, inputting, and otherwise managing information—created and communicated by others within the organization. Many of us perform transaction work as part of our daily routine: booking travel plans on an Internet page or providing Human Resources with personal information on a self-service intranet site. This is a vital part of increasing the productivity factor for the entire enterprise but should remain a minimal part of the work routine for brokers, experts, or integrators. As we see in the I-Work distribution

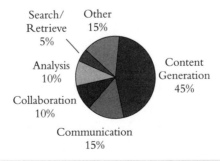

FIGURE 2.6   I-Work Distribution: Transactors

model for transactors, data entry personnel, functional analysts, and the like spend the majority of their work time, translating information from one format to another.

TRANSACTION I-WORKER PERSONA

Greg is in his first year as a financial analyst. He spends most of his workday collecting and organizing data, building internal reports with diagrams and charts, then making recommendations based on the data. Although Greg works independently, the research he does and documents he writes are dependent on instructions from his supervisor and information gathered from other sources.

Collaborators

Collaborators (or information brokers), such as departmental managers or professionals in large service firms, use information gleaned from experts and analysts, as well as their own expertise, to address the objectives of their organizations and to direct or coordinate with others effectively. Collaborators are the information brokers in the work scenario. As brokers, they heavily rely on collection tools and spend the majority of their time in meetings and communicating with others. This was the situation we found in the Air Force study, where we had a group of collaborators responsible for managing succession planning within the agency. The model we developed for our productivity impact studies calls for brokers to spend approximately 25 percent of their time collaborating with others and an additional 20 percent analyzing and solving problems. The results from the Air Force study indicated that 68 percent of the target group's work time was being expended in seeking or searching (through searching, communicating, or collaborating) for information and 20 percent was spent in content production. Of the total work time the AFSLMO team reported spending only 23 percent on collaborating and problem solving. A more productive work balance (as shown in Figure 2.7) for information coordinators, such as those in our study, would be content 20 percent, search activities 10 percent, communication 20 percent, collaboration/analysis 45 percent, and 5% on other (non–role specific activities).

COLLABORATIVE I-WORKER PERSONA

Mark is a marketing manager who supervises several other people. He spends almost twice as much time working with documents (mostly editing and correcting them) compared to any other activity. He also spends a large part of his time communicating via e-mail, phone, and in meetings. The rest of the day is consumed problem solving and planning. Since Mark is in charge, his primary role is to make sure other people use knowledge effectively to complete their tasks, but the information he needs to complete his own tasks is supplied by experts and analysts.

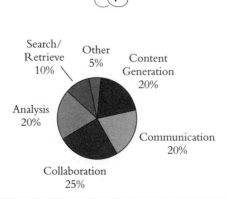

FIGURE 2.7 I-Work Distribution: Brokers

These I-workers depend on their ability to be in constant contact—using a variety of synchronous (two-way collaboration) techniques as well as the more traditional asynchronous means such as phone, e-mail, and other mobile computer devices—with coworkers, clients, and suppliers. Collaborators make knowledge-based decisions based on these team-oriented interactions.

Integrators

Integrators, such as dispatchers, nurses, or construction engineers, use technology and information to know how or when to complete predefined tasks with other team members. Their roles often involve a cross-functional and cross-organizational set of static procedures.

In the past decade or so, technological advances have rapidly spread into the more mobile of the integrator roles through devices such as cell phones and on-board computers. Integrators focus primarily on the performance of work scenarios based on information rather than on the creation or interpretation of information. The integrated worker represents not only the newest of information-centric role but the largest and fastest-growing group. From the BLS data shown in Figure 2.1, we easily see that the non–office-based workforce represents approximately 45 percent of all information-centric workers in the U.S. economy. A quick check of data from 2002 indicates that most of the information-centric job growth occurred in this category. The continued introduction of new technology that allows direct communication with field-based and virtual workers will continue to push this trend and change the nature of these roles. The I-work distribution for integrators is shown in Figure 2.8.

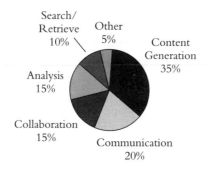

FIGURE 2.8 I-Work Distribution: Integrators

INTEGRATED I-WORKER PERSONA

Sally is an emergency medical dispatcher (EMD). Although Sally's EMD training taught her how to handle 911 calls, she also relies on a list of procedures that tell her specifically how to respond to certain situations. In addition to this set of instructions, she also has the assistance of an automated system used to quickly pinpoint the location of each caller. Sally spends the majority of her time fielding calls and dispatching emergency workers.

As technology continues to infiltrate all kinds of industries and drive the Information Age forward, we will see changes in the expert, transaction, collaborative, and integrated I-worker roles. The one constant will be the growing importance of the consistent flow of quality information in the creation of business value.

Reviewing how our two case study partners aligned the roles within their organizations helps to clarify why having a work–behavior alignment model can guide your improvement project. As we see in in Figure 2.9, which compares the U.S. Air Force case study example with the model, being out of alignment is costly. In the early stages of the study, all the succession planning team roles were identified as coordinators. The uniform nature of the workforce makes it easier to spot the alignment challenges.

Interestingly, over 60 percent of the Case Study 1 respondents reported that they used e-mail (personal communications) to exchange information. From our opportunity mapping, or top-down data collection and interviews, we discovered that e-mail was the major means of information exchange and sharing for succession planning documents and decisions. This heavy reliance on one-way communications tools explains the extensive use of advanced features of the e-mail application (revealed in the baseline study) and the strong concern that respondents expressed regarding e-mail reliability and speed. In such cases we see team members lobbying for increased mailbox size and applying great pressure on their organizations to invest in upgrades to e-mail systems.

An indicator of the reliance on e-mail as the primary communications tool was clear when 49 percent of the

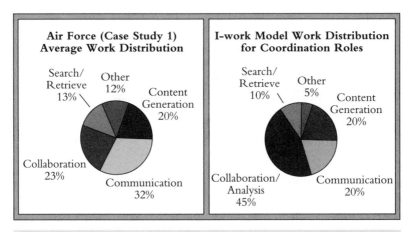

FIGURE 2.9   Work Distribution for Case Study 1 versus Model

group indicated they could not perform succession planning work when the e-mail systems are down. Luckily, 70 percent of the group saw less than four e-mail disruptions a year (88 percent as a result of server/network issues). If e-mail disruptions lasted one hour or less, the financial impact to the succession planning function for each disruption, if calculated in actual dollars, was approximately $70 hour/outage or $63,000/year in overtime. We recommended changing the work distribution to include more collaboration and intranet-based shared services to avoid these delays or work stoppages. The benchmark study conducted after improvements and procedure changes were implemented demonstrated a 47 percent decrease in the e-mail traffic with attachments. This not only eased the burden on an overtaxed e-mail system but actually helped the succession planning group exceed its work-effort reduction goals.

The broad nature of the Korean Air (Case Study 2) audience required all headquarters groups to be segmented and modeled, at a high level, before we could do a work distribution model. In general, most roles spent just over 30 percent of their effort on generating or managing output. After adjustments were made for cultural differences, the project team's recommendation was to slowly modify procedures as new technology was introduced into the environment. The technology renovation would provide an opportunity to refresh training on the advanced features of technology (e.g., Microsoft Word and Excel) that were underutilized and to redirect current behaviors that were resulting in lost efficiency with the goal of reducing the content generation time by 3 to 5 percent (on average across the workforce). The goal of this reduction was not time saved but improve process cycle efficiency—essentially the optimization of the Korean Air workflow.

CONCLUSION

Commercial and government organizations have been driving toward the improvement of information-centric productivity for the past two decades. In the United States, the Clinger-Cohen Act of 1996 requires government information technology (IT) to operate as efficiently and effectively as similar units within a commercial business. Managing productivity improvement programs brings new challenges to the already complicated landscape of technology oversight and contracting. Regulatory compliance issues have now been layered on top of the traditional challenges of complex systems management.

Establishing a Lean Six Sigma (LSS)[4] compliant Productivity Impact Framework program provides the means to clarify structure, goals, work procedures, and tools that can reduce conflicts and risk. In addition, the same framework provides process and procedure documentation that can reduce work exceptions (maintaining consistent business rules) and improves compliance with organizational documentation requirements.

Poor control of information and outdated infrastructure can lead to a potential loss of competitive advantage that can negatively influence both share price and revenue with unintended consequences on talent, productivity, and performance. An added benefit of providing clarity around work processes is the potential avoidance, in the worse cases, of unethical practices that have caused major disruption and financial loss in organizations such as Enron and Arthur Andersen.

Improving revenue is often an important aspect of measuring and managing productivity. A minor change in procedures coupled with a small investment in technology (under $40,000) allowed the Air Force team to gain that 14 percent improvement in work throughput. Savings such as these can allow for the reallocation of millions of dollars through improved cycle efficiency.

There is no doubt that building a structure for improving productivity can be profitable. Using that same structure to improve corporate compliance adds the kind of bonus the executive office often does not see. Building visibility for broad reaching processes and complex practices can be costly but often necessary not only for compliance but for business continuity. A recent study noted these costs related to Sarbanes-Oxley compliance:

- The average per-company Section 404 total implementation costs were estimated to be approximately $7.8 million, which represents approximately 1/10th of 1 percent of subject company revenues.
- Average per-company auditor fees were estimated to be approximately one-quarter of the total implementation costs, or 1/40th of 1 percent of Subject Company revenues.[5]

Establishing a productivity framework moves your organization from a reactive to a proactive compliance state. This is important as stakeholders, markets, and regulators have less tolerance for organizations that do not have adequate controls and procedures in place to document and clarify processes and practices. As with any transformation, there are no quick fixes. The solutions presented here are anchored on a comprehensive plan that develops a controllable and scalable infrastructure than can support the present and future strategies of the enterprise.

ENDNOTES

1. Founding sponsors of the Information Work Productivity Center include Accenture, Cisco, Intel, HP, Microsoft, SAP, and Xerox. Information Work Productivity Center academic participants include

Dale Jorgenson, Harvard, Kennedy School of Government, Director of the Program on Technology and Economic Policy; Erik Brynjolfsson, Co-Director, Center for eBusiness , M.I.T., Sloan School of Management, Baruch Lev, NYU, Stern School of Business, Director of the Vincent C. Ross Institute for Accounting Research; and Hal Varian, UC Berkeley, Haas School of Information Management and Systems, Dean. Jeff Raikes of Microsoft served as the chairman and Susan Conway as the executive director of the Council.

2. Tom Peters, "The Wow Project," Business 2.0, Issue 24 (May 1999): 116.

3. Information Work Productivity Center, Information Work Research Report (2004). This study, under Professor Vish Krishnan of the University of Texas, included 1,500 participants from 256 major companies. Many of the components of that study are used in the surveys and analysis used in the PIF model.

4. Six Sigma is a methodology that uses specific problem-solving approaches and tools to improve processes and products. The approach is data driven, with the goal of reducing unacceptable products or events. Technically Six Sigma is about reducing process variation, such as the number of errors per million lines of code or parts produced. In the information-centric world it is about reducing the rework, maintaining a consistent, secure, and reliable information flow in order to deliver the right answer.

5. "Sarbanes-Oxley Section 404 Costs and Remediation of Deficiencies: Estimates from a Sample of Fortune 1000 Companies," Charles River Associates, April 2005.

❧ 3 ❧

Realizing Value

Building an information productivity framework for your organization helps to visualize the invisible production line. Although we may not see it, every organization has an information production line. Technology is used to create, modify, and otherwise utilize information that in turn creates products or services for customers. This production line delivers tangible results that drive the business, such as tickets, work orders, or customer requests.

WHY MEASURE THIS PRODUCTION?

You may be thinking "We measure output, why measure the use of information?" If you owned a factory, would you measure and monitor the inventory going in against the finished products leaving? You can be assured that every business manager or owner would answer YES!

Unfortunately, if the traditional, manufacturing-based productivity equation is applied to information work (I-work), the result would be *zero,* or no productivity. This is because the output of I-work is not directly measurable, like the output of a manufacturing plant would be.

However, if you take a different view of I-work, there are definite and measurable productivity gains from increasing information flow efficiency. The I-work cost of production is generally listed as zero, leaving you with just the cost of labor to complete the equation. Ensuring that labor is properly channeled and supported is important to productivity. As we saw in Case Study 1, the Air Force study, the team noted that only 23 percent of their I-work was expended in building the solution (collaborating and problem solving); 32 percent of their I-work was spent on asynchronous (or one-way) communications. In other words, a large virtual workforce was leaving messages, rebuilding spreadsheets, and working very hard to complete their tasks with the tools at hand. Fixing the information flow by increasing the ability to collaborate improved the work structure and allowed the team to realize a 14 percent decrease in work effort. Understanding the nature of the information flow problem allows us to fix the invisible assembly line.

HOW DO WE MEASURE I-WORK PRODUCTION?

It is no longer the cost of production but the cost of enablement that generates information-based value. The formula for generating I-Work value is simple:

The right processes (similar to having
the right assembly line)
+
The right procedures (know-how on the line)
+
The right tools (technologies)
=
I-Work value generation

Modeling productivity within organizational boundaries establishes the intersection between ability, represented by functional roles, and capability, in the form of structured processes. The goal of the Productivity Impact Framework (PIF) and its measurement models is to find the optional points of efficiency and effectiveness for these intersections within a work scenario, department, or entire enterprise.

Creating an Image of I-Work Production

Creating an image of production allows us to make decisions about workflow improvement. Managing a business is not easy; we need tools to make decisions. As managers, we know new technology is always waiting to help make life easier. Unfortunately, we cannot invest in every improvement our team would like to try. Viewing the two PIF measurement models—Sigma scoring and the deeper Productivity Impact Measures (PIMs)—provides management guidance at a glance. The Sigma level (measured on a 1- to 6-point scale), process cycle efficiency (PCE) and Delivery velocity (the speed of and time taken to deliver) provide a snapshot view of the productivity health of the work scenario. If the Sigma scores are not satisfactory, a review of the PIM rating on work and technology alignment will provide a deeper understanding of the constraints within your think factory. The combined PIF measures allow managers to make improvement decisions with greater confidence of productively gains.

There is minimal downside to a productivity study. Even if you do not find great improvement opportunities, you will have documented your work scenarios, procedures, and deliverables. In essence, you will have built the core components of a business continuity plan. Considering the aging and transient nature of the workforce in many sectors and the volatile nature of the world economy today, creating such a plan should be part of every long-term business strategy.

The true upside of a productivity study is the potential for business growth and workplace improvement. No one can guarantee results, but the kinds of gains organizations have made are hard to ignore. Managers would like to report double-digit productivity gains, as we saw in the Air Force case study. That 14 percent throughput improvement is impressive, but many of us would be satisfied with the 3 to 4 percent improvement target set in the Korean Air case study. Improvements of this nature across a large organization can easily bring a million or two to the bottom line through improved output using the same or even a reduced workforce. Streamlining work scenarios often allows an enterprise to take advantage of natural workforce turnover (retirements and voluntary leave) to restructure work and eliminate non–value-added activities. Clearly defined work and information flows also open the door to virtual and global work distribution.

Restructuring, or streamlining, work requires a good roadmap. It is often difficult to build an image of how work is done without an expensive task analysis project. PIF provides a methodology for building a high-level roadmap by work scenario.[1] The PIF taxonomy creates a solid foundation for starting business continuity documentation, including workflow and value stream analysis. The organization can selectively drill down into poorly performing areas to drive out a detailed analysis. In government, where the leadership can change every few years, it is good stewardship of the public trust to provide documentation, management, and workflow roadmaps. Thus, even if the political winds change, productivity improvement plans will be understood and logically moved forward.

Measuring Work Scenario Health

The Lean Six Sigma guidance that underpins PIF focuses the reporting on process/procedure effectiveness (capability and alignment) and efficiency (ease of use and speed of delivery). The ultimate goal is to improve customer delivery. To this end, the measurements are structured to determine the sources of variation and time bottlenecks.

Measurement is a constant theme in PIF. Recalling the old adage that you can't manage what you can't measure, we not only need to have measures but we need to have a clear understanding of their meaning. Visualize PIF measures as a hierarchy as shown in the pyramid diagram

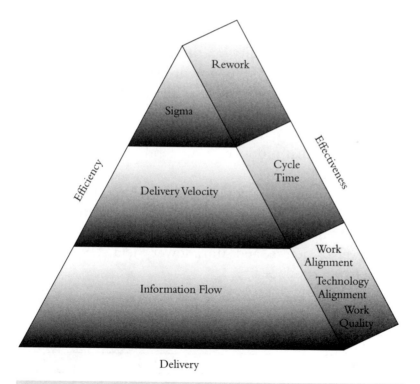

FIGURE 3.1 Productivity Impact Measurement Structure

(Figure 3.1). At the top of the measurement pyramid—the first indicator management needs to look at—is the Sigma indicator. In a manufacturing environment, the Sigma indicator points to the level of defects generated during a production process. Information-centric work does not generally present itself in a manner that allows us to count the defects in production. To build an image of variation in production, we need to look at:

- *Deliverables* (rework rate)
- *Efficiency* (of technology)
- *Effectiveness* (from work behaviors)

The Sigma indicator is a number between 1 and 6 that indicates the quality of delivery. In Lean Six Sigma terms, things that do not meet the customer's expectation (in terms of quality or timing) are defects. If you promise delivery of a document within two days and quality issues require you rework the content three times resulting in delivery on the third day, you have a defective workflow. Your I-work process is as defective as an assembly line that produces loose fenders on three out of every ten cars.

When we first looked at the Air Force team, we estimated its Sigma level at approximately 3 (at or greater than 93.32 percent effectiveness). A low Sigma level indicates a high level of defects and, thus, lower yield. The standard Sigma to yield values are:

Sigma Level	Yield
30.85%	1
69.15%	2
93.32%	3
99.38%	4
99.87%	5
99.99%	6

The difference in yield gets smaller as you increase the Sigma level. The scale takes a jump of more than 30% as you go from level 2 to level 3. But all levels above 4 are at a 99% or greater yield. Determining the Sigma levels of processes allows process performance to be compared across the enterprise because the Sigma level is a normalized view of the process. The Sigma level is simply a determination of opportunities—that is the opportunity of reduced defects. The Sigma level must, however, be expressed in terms that relate to the specific process. PIF develops measures against each major procedure (not task) within a given practice area (of a process). These measures can then be calculated at the procedure, practice and/or process level to provide summary level information or snap-shots of the opportunity potential.

Sigma Impact

The Sigma level is the first indicator of process/practice health. If the Sigma level indicator is unacceptable or if the gap is too large, the next meter to view is the delivery velocity, which is the second level of PIF measurement. Velocity, or the speed, at which deliverables are produced helps us focus on what creates long lead time. Little's Law (named for the mathematician who first provided the proof points) simply states that:

> In essence, Little's Law targets the development of an estimate of how long it takes something to cycle through the process from start to finish. The completion rate is very simply the number of deliverables produced in a given period of time.[2] Written simply as:
>
> Lead Time = Total Work in Process / Average Completion Rate

Examining the delivery velocity at the work scenario level gives us a good indication of overall delivery speed. To increase velocity, you need to eliminate waste (time traps) or non–value-added procedures. Wasted time (in a process) is

generally associated with rework or time spent waiting for a
response from others associated with the process (e.g., a
supervisor or manager). Applying the old 80/20 rule, we
could say that 80 percent of the time spent in nonoptimized
procedures is a result of waiting for people or information.[3]

The Air Force case study presented us with a Sigma indicator level that was passable but a process that was consuming
too much time in production. The team was running 10- and
11-hour days (consistent overtime) to produce the required
deliverables.

Delivery flow can also be viewed in terms of the
process cycle time. A lean, world-class process is one in
which the value added time is no more than 25 percent of
the total lead time. Process Cycle Efficiency (PCE) provides another snap shot of efficiency within a given procedure and can be calculated at the practice if all the major
procedure data has been collected and at a process level if
all the major practices have been measured. PCE is simply
expressed as:

$$PCE = Value\ Add\ Time/Lead\ Time$$

A PCE of 10% or less should indicate a strong opportunity for improvement. Additional discussion and Case
Study examples of PCE can be found in Chapter 6.

Poor Sigma rating, delivery velocity and/or PCE indicators are statistical signals that we need to examine the I-work
flow variables that can be adjusted to improve the situation.

PRODUCTIVITY IMPACT MEASURES

Productivity impact measures (PIM), used in PIF, produce
a more subjective/quality view of information flow and
technology utilization. PIM provides us with a quantitative
view of the variables that impact our ability to do I-work:

work behaviors, work distribution, technology alignment, and utilization.

The PIM shown in Figure 3.2 provides an overview of the results for the Air Force study (Case Study 1). This PIM gives us a visual image of the information flow variables that might affect the quality and cycle time of the work scenario being studied.

The information flow index provides guidance when you start to work on improvement plans. Improvements in work distribution are often linked to changes in the supporting technology. As hand-in-glove issues, it is critical to make sure one continues to support the other. The Air Force team found that the way it was working (work distribution) was out of alignment with the collaborative roles members were assigned. The work alignment and technology utilization indexes for this study, shown in Figure 3.2, helped the project team to understand why the delivery velocity indicators were low. In June 2005 the work alignment index for the succession planning group was at 30 percent, indicating that compared to the PIF model for collaborators, the majority of the work activities were out of alignment. This fact indicated that I-workers were using an outdated (or incorrect) approach to the work required

Productivity Impact Measures Human Resources Functions	Work Alignment- June '05 (%)	Technology Alignment- June '05 (%)	Work Alignment- January '06 (%)	Technology Alignment- January ë06 (%)
Succession Planning	30	75	70	80

FIGURE 3.2 Air Force Case Study: Productivity PIM

to accomplish the tasks. Their technology utilization, at 75 percent, was not overly challenging but low enough to warrant investigation. Realigning the work effort was not possible without changes to the supporting technology. Using existing technology licenses, the project team was able to build an intranet support site that allowed the group to increase collaborative work by nearly 74 percent. This not only changed the way team members worked but improved delivery speed, reducing the labor hours by 14 percent.

Improvement planning is the end goal of productivity assessment. Keep in mind one basic goal when considering the action plans: Improve output.

Where to Look for Value?

Our experience over the past three years has pointed out that these financial measures are good to gauge the value of I-work improvements:

- Changes to budget expense show significant correlation with reduction in cycle times.
- Improvements in operating excellence show significant correlation to increases in the percent of work completed on time.
- Improvements in return on assets (ROA) show correlation to increases in work quality.
- In addition, changes to the cost of production show correlation to
  - Project cycle times
  - Project costs
  - Percent of projects completed on time[4]

CONCLUSION

In the twentieth century, many western countries made the shift from agricultural economies to industrial economies and finally to technology-based information economies. As intriguing as this shift is in developed economies such as the United States or western Europe, there is a much larger opportunity available in examining currently developing countries. In the coming years, an untold number of workers in parts of Asia, the Far East, Latin America, and Africa will make this same shift. John Naisbitt, in his 1995 book, *Global Paradox,* surveys the major economic trends and observes what he calls the "global paradox" at work.[5] That is, as the world becomes vastly more integrated, Naisbitt notes, the small, agile, and informed players will profit the most.

The questions that we must all ponder in the coming months and years include a careful examination of the role that information and I-work will play in the new economy. Is connectivity, collaboration, and/or knowledge exchange the key to business success in the Information Age? If information-bound activities are the key to business success, do collaborative and connectivity technologies become more important? Companies that focus their activities on examining I-work and determining how to provide solutions that drive I-worker productivity will be in a position to improve their own productivity, foster stronger relationships with their customers and partners, and stay ahead of their competition. Today's businesses need to take advantage of this huge opportunity to lead the charge toward more productive I-work and stronger economies. Ultimately, the Information Age will be measured not by the output of technological products but by the improvement of the actions and decisions that drive business performance.

ENDNOTES

1. A work scenario is the natural flow of work regardless of the organizational boundaries. A work scenario for procurement contracts might include I-workers from the purchasing, legal, and sales departments. Each set of I-workers might add a unique procedure or two to the work scenario or simply participate in one or more of the core procurement work procedures. Regardless of the work composition, most work scenarios are composed of matrix teams that deliver multiple outputs.

2. Little's Law, as in queuing theory, says: *The average number of customers in a stable system (over some time interval) is equal to their average arrival rate, multiplied by their average time in the system.* The law was named for John Little based on results of experiments in 1961.

3. The Pareto Principle states that for many phenomena, 80 percent of consequences stem from 20 percent of the causes. It is named after Italian economist Vilfredo Pareto but was framed by management thinker Joseph M. Juran.

4. We validated these correlations through a sponsored study with Professor Vish Krishnan, University of Texas, in 2005 across 1,500 participants from 256 major companies. Many of the components of that study are used in the surveys and analysis used in the PIF model.

5. Naisbitt, John, Global Paradox, Avon Books, 1995.

Part Two

FOCUSING ON VALUE

Passion for reinvention and streamlining has historically driven innovation in business and public life. Ever since Eli Whitney revolutionized American manufacturing with the introduction of the assembly line, U.S. business and many public sector leaders have worked to boost organizational productivity. They have sought to reduce waste, eliminate unnecessary labor costs, and correct poorly conceived or inefficient work approaches. The next frontier for improving work productivity is in the area of optimized information flow. While technology has delivered significant and documented productivity improvements in the manufacturing sector of the economy, information work (I-work) is in the rudimentary stages of being mapped, measured, and managed—a task hindered by the intangible and diverse nature of information processing. Previously, information management was measured solely by analyzing the amount an organization (or an economy) spends on technology, without an understanding of the impact of that technology on performance.

Improving productivity requires measurement. Through the Productivity Impact Framework (PIF) and the associated Productivity Impact Measures (PIM), we have established the essential elements of performance measurement:

- Standard activities (work behaviors/types)
- Materials (information)
- Structure (process/practice/procedure/roles)
- Value (deliverables)

The final requirement for performance measurement is to establish a baseline consisting of the ideal state of performance and compare this to the current state. Part II of this book focuses on the mechanism for collecting and analyzing the performance data. We round out this picture in Part III with a discussion on establishing the cost benefits of improvement. Although many executives want the benefit statements up front, it is important to remember that a good cost-benefit analysis starts with solid performance measures. A Productivity Opportunity Map (POM) is initiated at the beginning of each assessment to ensure that we are addressing the right targets within the organization. A POM allows the team to provide estimates of the potential benefits and set initial improvement targets before the project addresses the full audience of information workers and managers.

The input and output for I-work is often the most intangible of assets—*information or an information-based product*. It is therefore critical to measure the use, flow, and distribution of information through the virtual assembly line.

Moving from theory to action requires a plan. PIF as a plan of action was initiated as a joint effort between the U.S. Air Force and Microsoft Consulting Services to shape the evolving methodology into a repeatable, scalable means and demonstrate the benefit created through the implementation of current and future changes to the work environment. Most public and private enterprises see that one of the richest opportunities to gain improvement is in I-work or the front end of the business: the offices, service areas, and support processes required to operate a business or service agency. In many instances, these functions face both efficiency and effectiveness challenges. I-work activities are often among the least optimized of business functions. While many back-end functions (repair facilities, inventory, and the like) have successfully applied Lean Six Sigma (LSS) production as well as a variety of other methods and tools to streamline their process, the lack of effective I-work streamlining has left front-end processes struggling to improve effectiveness and efficiency. PIF supports and uses the LSS (*define-measure-analyze-improve-control*) structure shown in Figure PII.1. This model provides structure for the baseline needs of productivity improvement projects. Collecting the right data and analyzing it are critical steps. Central to PIF is the ability to point out the potential for eliminating tasks that may be non–value-added or unnecessary from an overall productivity perspective. PIF also demonstrates where and when technology might be added to improve productivity. Figure PII.2 provides the details for the five phases model.

In the next three chapters we discuss how to target and structure a productivity assessment program. The first challenge, tackled in Chapter 4, is to determine where within the enterprise and on what work scenario to target the assessment. Once we have our target, Chapter 5 outlines the basic plan of action called for by PIF that then allows us

FIGURE PII.1 PIF LSS/DMAIC Model

Phase	Action	Description	Project Work
1	Define	Defines the problem or opportunity in a process or procedure that affects the procedural require-ment or specifications.	Produce a project vision/scope statement and complete an Oppor-tunity Map to gather a sufficiently deep set of data followed a Baseline Assessment (that will also require data from the Measure phase).
2	Measure	Defines and identifies key measurements, data collection plan and presents a statistical conclusion for the specified characteristics and/or level of opera-tion based on the observed data collected. The actual assessment and data collection maybe outsourced to a vendor.	Use the value stream analysis to identifiy the procedures used in the assessment (survey) tool. If adequate procedures do not exist (in the current survey), then they will need to be built (as described in "Structuring Baseline Measures"). Once measures are identified, a measurement analysis approach (how data will be collected) is imple-mented and the data collection effort is launched.

Phase	Action	Description	Project Work
3	Analyze	Process, procedure, or service details are reviewed for process improvement opportunities. This portion of the process may be handled by a vendor and managed to the specification set out by the project team.	Data collected during the measure phase is used to create a gap analysis report. The results of the gap analysis allow the team to complete the improvement roadmap. This data also serves as the baseline upon which an RFP can be written.
4	Improve	Defines where solutions and ideas may be generated and ruled on. Once a problem has been successfully identified, measured, and analyzed for gaps, the results can be evaluated to fill gaps.	Improvement plans are launched to fill productivity gaps or improve efficiency. Baseline measures associated with the gap are isolated for reassessment in the benchmark studies
5	Control	Establishing a program of continuous improvement requires follow up measurement (benchmarking) to record success or failure of the program.	A critical step for performance improvement projects is measuring the key performance indicators (KPIs) to ensure the critical success factors(CSFs) for the program are met.

to produce the PIM or measures described in some detail in Chapter 6.

Before starting our planning discussion, here is another case study we can refer to.

CASE STUDY 3: BUILDING INFORMATION STRUCTURES IN FINANCIAL SERVICES (APRIL 2006)

Like Korean Air (Case Study 2), this financial institution set out to create an enterprise-wide improvement plan. The target was to improve the flow of information across and through the various internal and external organizations that make up its vast network of employees, suppliers, and customers linked together to provide and/or consume financial transactions. This major U.S. financial enterprise wanted to identify its I-work taxonomy and begin to establish a productivity baseline for its 35,000+ person information-centric workforce. The taxonomy, the first output of an impact study, was to be used to link the various business units to the new enterprise portal. First, using the PIF methodology, the team guided the leadership in a top-down opportunity mapping exercise. The exercise interviewed subject matter experts in the target functional areas and established common and unique procedures across this diverse worker audience focusing on two areas, use of information (the action) and purpose of the procedure (the object). No concept development is without its challenges. This team encountered a few of them with the PIF project as it struggled with its first pilot group in defining this critical step in taxonomy definition. Chapters 4 and 5 presents more information on the issues this group encountered and the unique solutions it is discovering as it adjusts PIF to its corporate culture. Since this is a unique and far-reaching project, the improvement cycle is long—two to three years in this case. We will talk about a number of challenges and setbacks the team has encountered in its team building and project definition. This case study, along with Case Study 1 and Case Study 2, highlights the setup and execution of PIF projects.

❧4❧

Structuring the Measurement Environment: Where and What to Measure

Business performance is driven from the external indicators of success: market value for commercial enterprises or the budget, or tax dollar, investment for public agencies. Some organizations systematically outperform others. The list of superperformers crosses all industries and sectors: Wal-Mart in retail, Dell in computer hardware, IBM in computers and related services, Microsoft in software, Intel in semiconductors, DuPont in chemicals, UPS and FedEx in shipping, Goldman Sachs in investment banking, and Southwest in airlines. We could continue this list for several pages, but the goal is to understand what allows these enterprises to stand out from the crowd and outperform their peers. The hallmark of these star performers is long-term growth in sales, earnings, and market value. Looking at the abbreviated list of star performers, we can say their above-average return on investment is not a result of a lack of competition. Rather their success is directly related to the organization of the enterprise. Enterprises such as Wal-Mart and Southwest Airlines sit squarely in the middle of extremely competitive markets. These enterprises have driven up the value of an intangible asset that is often referred to as *organization capital.*

PRODUCTIVITY IN A COMPETITIVE WORLD

Examples of specific business processes and designs that are components of organization capital include the following:

1. Wal-Mart's supply chain, where the reading of the barcodes of purchased products at the checkout register is directly transmitted to suppliers who are in turn largely responsible for inventory management and product provision to the thousands of Wal-Mart stores;

2. Cisco's Internet-based product installation and maintenance system, estimated by Cisco's CFO to have saved $1.5 billion over three years.[1]

3. Dell's pioneering built-to-order distribution system, where customers design their products; and

4. Toyota's streamlined and automated manufacturing;

5. Merck's extensive network of hundreds of R&D and marketing alliances and joint ventures, aimed at facilitating technology transfer and risk-sharing.[2]

The flow and utilization of information is the key component of organization capital. This key component, which Robert Solow, who's work in 1987 on economic growth earned him the Nobel Prize in economics, identified as the "residual", relates specifically to business processes and procedures. In essences, the secret sauce that makes market super performers is directly related to how information flows and is productively assimilated by their information workers (I-workers). Even research projects, which dynamically develops knowledge, must be translated into the think factory for it to become part of the recipe.

Information work (I-work) expressed as organization capital is often the only factor of production that is unique to a firm that is capable of yielding returns above the cost of capital.[3] Most other factors of production (labor and capital in particular) are commodities. Although the resource may become a baseline requirement to operate, such as electronic inventory management in large retail operations, it quickly loses its status as a competitive advantage. Large discount retailers like Kmart had access to the same labor pool and capital markets as the star performer in the field Wal-Mart. Kmart had equal access to technology vendors and external consultants. Yet the Wal-Mart team used the resources to outperform Kmart, who continued to loose market share. Certainly this is a simplistic description of the events, as there were a number of other factors, but it points out the value of organization capital in creating and sustaining star economic performers. In the information-centric economy, optimized information flow is the major value creator of business enterprises.[4] Essentially, what sets you apart from the competition is how you employ your physical resources and the optimized business methods you develop for your workforce.

The Productivity Impact Framework (PIF) methodology is designed to answer the challenge of measuring the state of the information flow at the operational level, as shown in Figure 4.1. Business leaders and consultants in search of the status of organization capital within an enterprise, specifically the human capital side of the equation, will find some answers in PIF. Models of operational measurement can be achieved if the time is taken to link the state of the information flow to the more traditional business measures (e.g., return on assets or equity) through enterprise key performance indicators (KPIs). Organization capital starts at the bottom of the enterprise food chain—the flow and use of information within the work scenario—and shows up in the financial results.

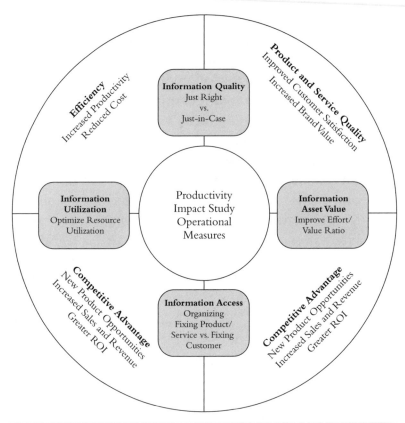

FIGURE 4.1 Components of Operational Measurement

ANALYZING INFORMATION FLOW

An analysis of a standard set of metrics for the flow of information allows decision makers to identify and map intangible asset utilization within groups or departments or across the whole organization.

It would be useful to refresh our definition of productivity at this point. For the purposes of this discussion, we can say productivity is the ratio of inputs to outputs, or simply the value of what you put into a process compared to what you get out of it. We are still talking about the three main components mentioned earlier: labor, capital (equipment, buildings, etc.), and other inputs (e.g., goods and purchased services).

These inputs are then divided by costs. The productivity improvement target for information-centric organizations is derived from an examination of labor productivity (value-added output per employee) as opposed to capital productivity (value-added output per dollar of capital stock).

It is logical to say that a company that has higher productivity will enjoy greater profitability. Profitability is generated by either producing the same output with fewer inputs, resulting in a cost advantage, or producing more, or better, output with the same inputs for a higher price. There is a paradigm associated with this model: Success attracts competition that will require even greater productivity.[5] Essentially we are looking at a continuing spiral or never ending race to gain customer loyalty through the production of better, faster and/or cheaper product. In the public sector, an agency that has greater productivity will realize higher operational efficiency. Operationally efficient enterprises produce the same, or more, output with fewer inputs to gain a lower cost of operation. Highly optimized operations are more successful in operating within budget limitations and are better able to respond when faced with budget cuts.

Fundamentally, organizations process information to coordinate and control output activity. The concepts of information processing optimization, for most organizations, has evolved over nearly a hundred years. That is most organizations are generally structured in a hierarchical manner whereas work is more likely to be done in a matrix fashion, as shown in Figure 4.2. The traditional model sees an organization as an information processing engine with a communications system, structured to achieve a set of specific tasks. Tasks are nested in organized procedures that are, in turn, executed by information processors (people, individually or in teams). People send and receive messages along the organizations predefined lines of communication, according to set rules and structures, using specific or ad hoc tools (e.g., e-mail, phone, or web-based portals).

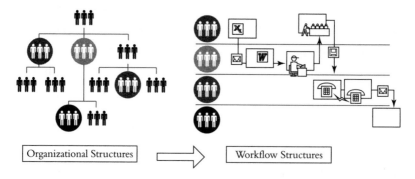

FIGURE 4.2   Traditional Work Structures

This model of operation provides a starting, or reference, point for the PIF model. Unlike business process reengineering approaches, PIF is an impact model. It looks at the impact of activities, behaviors, and technology on the information used to accomplish a result in a focused area of work. The PIF organizational image is different from the information processing model in Figure 4.2 in that it is more concerned with the optimization of the sender-receiver relationship, as shown in Figure 4.3, than with the optimization of the content of the messages contained in the flow.

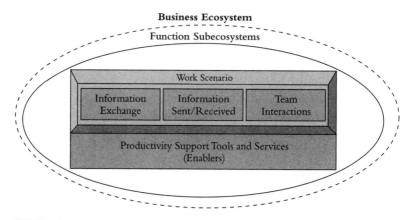

FIGURE 4.3   Ecosystem I-Work Structure

In the PIF model, the flow of information through the structured procedures defines the think factory assembly line. Measuring activity and utilization in this invisible assembly line requires a means of visualizing the activity. Building a process and practice taxonomy map allows the organization to validate that the productivity assessment is aimed at the correct work scenario. To achieve this goal a taxonomy, or map, of the specific portion of the ecosystem needs to be developed.

Once taxonomy has been established the team can build the more detailed opportunity map (as shown in Chapter 6). Tuning the elements of the procedures that are exposed in the opportunity map allows us to improve the productivity of the overall work scenario and the corresponding organizational capital. Taking this approach, we can examine both work effectiveness (e.g., the ability to access and acquire information) and work efficiency (e.g., the degree to which tools and technology support the work) because the ingredients (e.g. the behaviors such as develop or design) are the same. All four role categories—experts, brokers, transactors, and integrators—and modes of work—content generation, communication, collaboration, search and analysis—described in Chapters 2 and 3 can be seen as standard facilitators or operators within the information flow. Using this vision, we can model the amount of information being processed, or to be processed, by establishing a velocity of the desired deliverable. In PIF, a deliverable represents the output of a given procedures. Output can be physical deliverables (e.g., a document or design), a communication (e.g., an order or e-mail message), or collaboration (e.g., a meeting or review). This view is consistent and helps us model the contents of a procedure without having to disclose or expose actual content or a specific person.

BUILDING A WORK
SCENARIO STRUCTURE

Analyzing the gap between the desired state and actual work scenario operation is the key to discovering the value stream. The value stream is a representation of a fully efficient and effective work scenario—one that delivers the output within the desired time and specification (quality) with little, or no, rework. Work scenarios within a PIF model are described not only terms of their value but their connectivity to the enterprise. Each work scenario is connected to a basic navigational thread: process and practice (some practices may contain more than one work scenario). Once connected to the enterprise, the work scenario is then described in terms of its procedure, the work performed, and the technology used to accomplish the work. The PIF value equation is focused on the deliverable(s) produced by each value stream, or work scenario. The connectivity to the enterprise allows the PIF analyst to help business leaders determine not only if the work scenario is efficient but also if it is effectively contributing to the organizational goals and objectives. Essentially, all procedures must have value generating deliverables and all deliverables should contribute (directly or indirectly) to customer value.

When designing the targets for a productivity impact assessment for Korean Air (Case Study 2), as shown in Figure 4. 4, a horizontal approach that crossed all processes was chosen. The work scenario focus was corporate communications, which encompasses accessing and entering/ updating enterprise-level data, including human resources information, corporate financial and strategic data, as well as general person-to-person connectivity. The horizontal study required identifying the processes and practices that were most heavily impacted by the flow of corporate-level

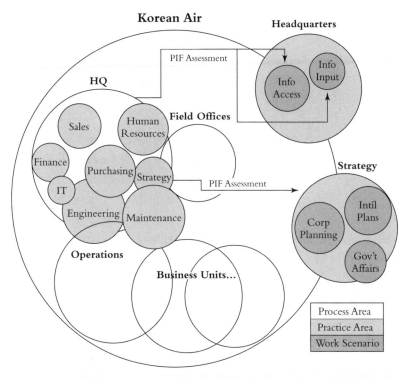

FIGURE 4.4 Korean Air Navigational Taxonomy

information. The search was narrowed to workgroups associated with the headquarters organization of the parent company. The next challenge was to determine the procedures commonly performed by the target audience. Korean Air's main goal was to improve the transparency and business utilization of corporate information. A work scenario was formed focused on the ability to access, find, and input required corporate data.

Measuring productivity in information-centric environments can be difficult. The key to production in these environments is the enablement of the I-worker in the performance of work scenarios and the production of key deliverables. The PIF approach takes a unique view into the nature of work scenarios as well as the means to build significant metrics around this critical intangible asset base. One means of improving productivity is tuning the procedures within the value stream to reduce the turbulence in the information flow. Procedure tuning, or streamlining, is accomplished by measuring the capability of the business rules and tools (technology) to support the I-worker in delivering the required output. The first thing a company must do to improve its productivity is to establish which work scenarios have the biggest impact on the economics of its ecosystem (e.g., as strategy planning). Then the company must identify the linkage between the outcomes of the work scenarios and the key measures of enterprise performance. The impact studies should help to identify where there are performance lags within the target work scenarios. These performance lags represent a gap that must be closed before an organization can become a star performer.

This brings us back to the essence of the PIF. Work occurs at the union of the five strategic taxonomies: navigational (structure), behavioral (work activities), roles (work types), enablers (technology and training), and deliverables (goals).

It is at the intersection, highlighted in Figure 4.5, that we measure productivity. The confluence of information consumption and information production within a work scenario represents a critical productivity point. If there are barriers, such as turbulence in the information flow, production is impeded. The ultimate goal is to streamline information-based work to optimize the production of customer deliverables. Productivity that generates profitability comes from optimizing work scenarios that in turn produce an end user deliverable, such as a legal contract, a mortgage loan, an overnight package delivery, or a company annual report. By identifying needed business processes or organizational changes by roles (people), business functions, and work products, businesses can prioritize process and organizational changes to maximize productivity when producing

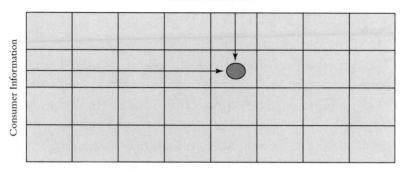

FIGURE 4.5 Taxonomy Union

Source: Image designed by Nikhil S. Shringarpurey, National City Corporation, April 2006.

customer or end user deliverables. The objective of a productivity impact study is to measure the velocity of information flow and the effect of that velocity on the quality of delivery.

Depending on your goals, you will choose either a horizontal or a vertical study plan. Horizontal studies look at work scenarios that cross multiple process areas, such as human resources, development and sales, or multiple practice areas within a single process, such as marketing, field sales, and invoicing within the sales process. Vertical studies limit their investigations to just one practice area, such as marketing, within a process area, such as sales.

Horizontal studies allow you to examine the information flow across large audiences. These studies are generally targeted at topics such as corporate communications or knowledge transfer, which have broad organizational impact. Vertical studies allow for in-depth investigation of a single area within the enterprise. Since the results of studies are quantitative, it is possible to aggregate the results of multiple vertical studies upward to build a summary image of entire process or practice. Whether you build the summary image first and, if needed, drive down to in-depth views or construct the process image from in-depth studies will depend on your project goals.

In the design phase of the horizontal study for Korean Air, diagramed in Figure 4.4, it became clear that unique communications-related issues were impeding information flow in some key functional areas. These challenges were centered on decision-making capability. A vertical assessment in corporate strategy was designed to operate in parallel with the corporate communications impact study. It is important to keep goals clearly in mind as you identify your assessment targets. Taking a broad horizontal approach that presents I-workers with a large number of questions on topics that may not relate to their work will tend to confuse and defocus the effort. If you choose a horizontal path, you may need, as Korean Air discovered, multiple vertical assessments to explore unique challenges. Korean Air's assessment program was unique in that the strategy group received a combined assessment (with both horizontal and vertical procedures) while the remaining groups received only the horizontal assessment. The result of the combined program was very successful. As Mr. S. M. Lee, Vice President and chief information officer of Korean Air, said, "...[the] survey and recommendations were very helpful for our study of employee productivity enhancements as well as the design of [the new] groupware system migration." You will read more about the development of this assessment program and the outcomes in the next few chapters.

The basic unit of work for an information flow analysis is the procedure level that represents the actual work level. Procedures are linked to the organization in two ways: first to the navigational structure of the organization by their association with processes and practices, and second by their connection to one or more deliverables that roots procedures firmly to value proposition for the organization. We can see this linkage in Figure 4.6, which diagrams the organizational assessment target for Case Study 1. In this vertical study we first determined the organizational structure within which the colonel management practice resided—human resources (HR)— and within HR in the Air Force Senior Leadership Management Organization (AFSLMO). The colonel management practice area contained three work scenarios: game planning (building and managing the lists of candidates), contender management (focused on the intervention and development), and the colonel assignment board (CAB). The three work scenarios are connected, as a practice, on the development and promotion of colonels within the Air Force. They share personnel and leadership but operate in a somewhat independent manner. The vertical assessment you will read about in the next chapters centered on the game planning work scenario. This scenario has a defined end point

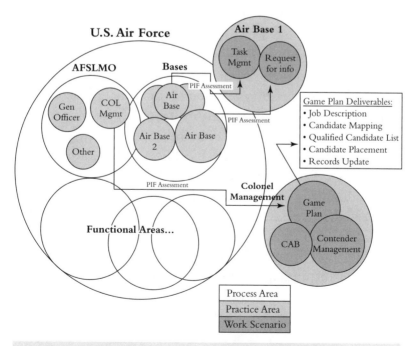

FIGURE 4.6 U.S. Air Force Navigational Taxonomy Sample

deliverable (new assignments) and a number of subdeliver-
ables that build up to a specific end point deliverable.
Clearly the assignment of colonels to new posts on a routine basis is critical to the smooth operation of the Air
Force. The end point deliverable has a defined timetable,
making it possible to measure velocity and map the
improvement to Air Force KPIs.

CONCLUSION

Measuring productivity at the point of work has a number
of challenges. Productivity challenges have numerous
causes including the need to rework deliverables and
exception handling. Finding the root cause of rework can
be it's own challenge and may include inconsistent information (from poorly structured requests to incorrect data),
unskilled I-workers, or aging tools that no longer deliver
information efficiently or effectively. Given the dynamic
nature of work in information-centric organizations, a
value stream analysis will need to look not only at breaks in
the flow causing rework but also the impedance caused by
exceptions (to common practice or procedural rules).
When the number of exceptions increases, productivity is
impacted. Exceptions serve as an indicator to managers that
something has shifted in the workflow. When impedance
occurs, regardless of the cause, an agile successful organization responds by making changes.

Now that we have looked at the taxonomy designed by
the Korean Air and the U.S. Air Force teams, we are set to
examine, in Chapter 5, how their assessment programs
were built for the targeted work scenarios.

ENDNOTES

1. *Economist,* June 26, 1999, p. 12.

2. Baruch Lev and Suresh Radhakrishnan, paper: "The Measurement of Firm-Specific Organizational Capital," New York University, Stern School, 2003.

3. As noted in ibid., even research and development yields, on average, the cost of capital. Chan et al. (2001) reported that the performance of firms conducting R&D is not superior, on average, to that of firms without R&D. See also Hall (1993) for similar results.

4. Lev and Radhakrishnan, "Measurement of Firm Specific Organizational Capital."

5. McKinsey Global Institute, "Synthesis of Findings Across Sectors, November 2002.

∞5∞

Measuring, Metering, and Monitoring the Information Flow

The focal point of productivity measurement is the collection of relevant data points from information workers (I-workers) within an enterprise to establish the health of the work scenario. It is the premise of the Productivity Impact Framework (PIF) model that a well-supported flow of quality information allows an information-centric organization (or group within a larger enterprise) to succeed at its mission. Since information work (I-work) cannot be measured directly in the same way as products moving down a physical assembly line, we need to look at the factors around the flow of information required to build a picture of its flow. Analyzing I-work is a multidimensional issue involving all elements of the work ecosystem: people, processes, technology, deliverables, and customers.

There needs to be a way to view, from the perspective of the I-worker, the operational flow of information through an organization. Visualizing information flow (amount, quality, and cycle time) through the enterprise (business processes/functions/activities) as it is managed, created, used, and transferred by the people performing the various roles and supported by the technology/services embedded in the infrastructure provides us with multidimensional pictures of the information assembly line.

The core focus of this measurement is building an AS–IS (baseline) and TO–BE (projected benefits) models. These models help managers, I–workers, and vendor teams capture, collaborate, and use business knowledge to efficiently design solutions that include their related operational requirements. These requirements include topology, business needs, and resources. Key objectives of the program are:

- Making a more "operationally aware" and holistic environment with technologies that leverage knowledge and are suited for a complex and constantly changing information technology (IT) environment, such as collaboration, content management, and secure searching.

- Engaging easy–to–use, scalable, model–based tools that cover every aspect of the information experience and leverage knowledge to provide flexible and agile business performance, a high level of automation end to end, the ability to incorporate best practices, and the capability to dynamically allocate resources based on changing business needs.

Once a program is established and a baseline is collected, an improvement plan can be proposed. Initiatives that drive efficiency and effectiveness in the target environment demonstrate the Lean Six Sigma (LSS) characteristics discussed earlier: solid *definition*, well-aligned *measures*, structured *analysis*, efficient *improvement* plans, and feedback/reassessment to validate improvements for *control* (DMAIC).

LSS-based programs can be applied to all processes, from manufacturing, software, operations, and transactions, to service providers. They accomplish the twin objectives by accounting for two perspectives: requirements that are critical to the customer and satisfying those requirements at the lowest possible cost.

BUILDING THE TEAM

Developing assessment programs and associated metrics requires a multidimensional team including personnel who understand the culture and business requirements of the organization and have expertise in data collection tools/ techniques and data analysis, statistics, and economics. Though not all skills are needed on a full-time basis, all are required to develop an effective productivity improvement plan. Contractors and outside research firms can be added to internal resources to fill some of roles on the core team. Figure 5.1 shows the team structure and relationship between the productivity core team and the opportunity (group to be assessed) field teams.

The core team consists of resources in these roles:

- *Program manager.* Ensures that business interests are represented; drives the overall programs to meet the business goals of the enterprise; provides business knowledge and thought leadership
- *Project manager.* Manages projects on a daily basis to meet the goals of delivering the solution within project constraints, provides project guidance
- *Technology lead.* Responsible for technical support for data repository and reporting, interfaces with the IT unit; provides technical expertise

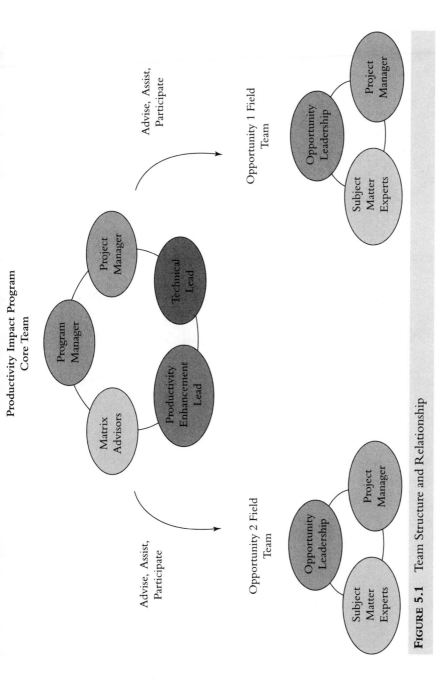

FIGURE 5.1 Team Structure and Relationship

- *Productivity enhancement lead* (highly recommended for programs with broad scope and enterprise-wide reach). Responsible for communicating organizational goals and supporting groups in forming productivity goals; assisting with the value chain analysis, supporting procedural changes, and providing process guidance; knowledgeable in organizational design
- *Matrix advisors.* Available to advise with critical issues (contract, budget, finance, legal) throughout the development process

For each selected opportunity, the business unit or field team consists of the following resources:

- *Opportunity leadership.* Provides thought leadership to the team
- *Project manager.* Co-manages the project with the core team, oversees the project on daily basis
- *Subject matter experts (SMEs).* Assist in the development of the baseline data in their functional areas

The appropriate team is essential to a successful project. In Case Study 3, participants struggled not only to launch their project but also to sustain the project through data collection due to a number of challenges, including a poor skill mix on the core team. This team took the time and effort to establish a solid scope statement and good executive sponsorship, but it failed to assign a balanced project team. This failure cascaded through the design and execution phases of the project—project management and communications became the critical weak links as the team failed to collect the appropriate data. The team lacked the experience to communicate the project to the managers, who in turn were unable to provide the appropriate support throughout their organizations. While a solid capable team is important in any team effort, it is essential to productivity improvement studies that rely on good lines of communication and a clear understanding by all participants.

HOW TO MEASURE

The Lean Six Sigma-Productivity Impact Framework (LSS-PIF) workflow model presented in Figure 5.2 provides a high-level overview of the steps involved in a productivity study and how they relate to the LSS phases.

A good roadmap is essential to completing any journey successfully. The pursuit of productivity is a continuous one filled with switchbacks that allow us to see the road already traveled. This view back gives us the opportunity to take note of our successes or take corrective action. Throughout this discussion we will reference the roadmaps and milestones in Figure 5.2. Each milestone or process step is described in Figure 5.3. The goal of this chapter is to take us through steps to identify the opportunity and establish a baseline.

Next we describe an approach to develop efficiency/effectiveness metrics for the identified opportunities. This approach helps to develop overall productivity trends by providing a snapshot assessment of the state of efficiency for the targeted work scenario(s). Over time, it will also help establish optimal operational levels and look ahead to tracking improvement progress. The approach consists of a slightly modified five-phase LSS process approach. As outlined in Figure 5.4, each phase has one or more outputs (deliverables) that are the result of a clearly identified set of outcomes. Organizations dedicated to improvement seek out the change opportunities. Clearly communicating this message at the outset of the program is central to the successful collection of good data. In Case Study 3, focused on a financial services company, the project team had identified

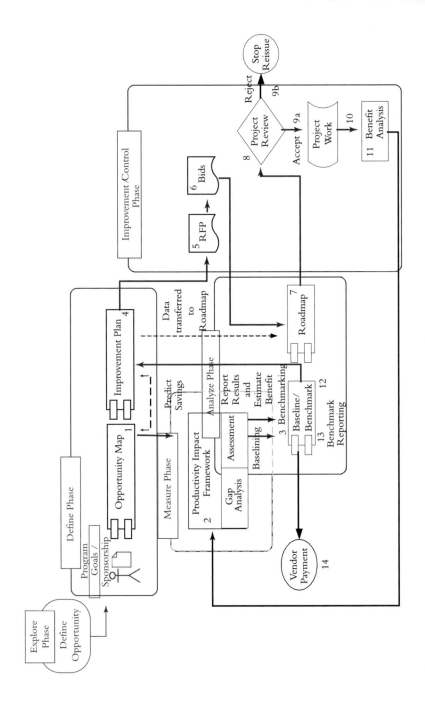

FIGURE 5.2 LSS–PIF Workflow Model

82

FIGURE 5.3 LSS-PIF Workflow Description

Step	Process	Description
1	Opportunity Mapping	A set of questions that assesses the proposed opportunity productivity potential in four areas: (1) technology efficiency, (2) technology effectiveness, (3) work delivery capability, and (4) work complexity. The results are incorporated into the PIF subjective and objectives measures for generating the baseline and estimating savings.
2	Productivity Impact Framework (PIF)	An approach to measure the productivity impact of changes to information-centric work in areas such as business rules, practices, technology enablers (e.g., hardware, software), procedures, and training. PIF defines major areas that a study takes on from gathering business information (costs, budget, current/planned technology, etc.) to assessment programs (measures of behaviors relating to I-work and information flow) that collect data on usage and operation needed for budget estimates, baseline and trending outputs. The PIF produces a baseline used for highlighting areas of productivity improvement across critical aspects of the work life cycle within the target business organization. Using baseline information and objective data, cost/saving estimates are calculated.
3	Baseline Report	A set of outputs derived from a productivity impact study from which variations are measured later. Outputs can include process measures (e.g., paper flow, adjudication), attribute measures (e.g., accuracy, customer satisfaction), and measures of efficiency (e.g., time). The baseline and estimates are incorporated into the roadmap component.

continues

FIGURE 5.3   LSS-PIF Workflow Description *Continued*

Step	Process	Description
4	Improvement Plan	The baseline report, plan and corresponding improvement roadmap are analytical models that outline the proposed program changes. This set of reports should outline the productivity gains, methods of achieving the gain and the risk factors, identification of a benefit (savings or enhanced revenue), and potential payback period for the plan. The business value calculations are manually developed (unless you use a vendor tool) using the results of the baseline report and vendor estimates to fulfill the change requirements of the change plan.
5	Request for Proposal (RFP)	A document that includes detailed information about the project requirements, specifications, baseline measures, and plans for improvement.
6	Bids	Invitations to bid are sent to the vendors.
7	Roadmap	A spreadsheet within the improvement plan designed for RFP responses to allow the team to compare potential solutions offered by vendors. The team should compare duration of the project, percent of gaps filled by the solution and cost. Once a solution is selected, the roadmap is created.
8	Project Review	Decision is based on subjective and objective data of the project. If accepted, project work is initiated, planned, and executed. Trend measures and benefit analysis are conducted using the PIF framework following the similar set of measures to arrive at the benchmark.
9a	Project Acceptance	
10	Project Work	
9b	Project rejection	Project is rejected.
	Stop/reissue	Project can be resubmitted with revisions.
11	Benefit Analysis	An analysis planning method of objective and subjective information used to determine improvement (based on the baseline).

Step	Process	Description
12	Benchmark Assessment	The same set of PIF measures are used to determine productivity gains and declare saving estimates.
13	Benchmark Report	Similar to a baseline report, benchmark reporting shows the improvement against the baseline. If a portion of the vendor pay is based on improving productivity the improvement benefits statement should be included in the benchmark report.
14	Vendor Payment	Based on contract agreement.

a solid project sponsor and met successfully with the operating managers, but failed to communicate the goals and approach of the data collection process to the target audience. The results were, of course, less than stellar. As we move through this chapter, we will parallel the experiences of this team with those of the teams in Case Studies 1 and 2, where the lines of communication were clear and the resulting deliverable was excellent.

DEVELOPING THE PROGRAM

Once the project has been staffed and the program sponsors have agreed to the program deliverables and timeline, the core team is ready to launch into the productivity study. The PIF workflow in Figure 5.2 provides a visual roadmap of the entire process image. For each program phase—explore, define, measure, analyze, and improve/control—the outlines provide a procedure breakdown diagram that includes a brief description of the success factors (deliverables), approach, and activities required of the team for the specific phase. This description is not meant as a complete

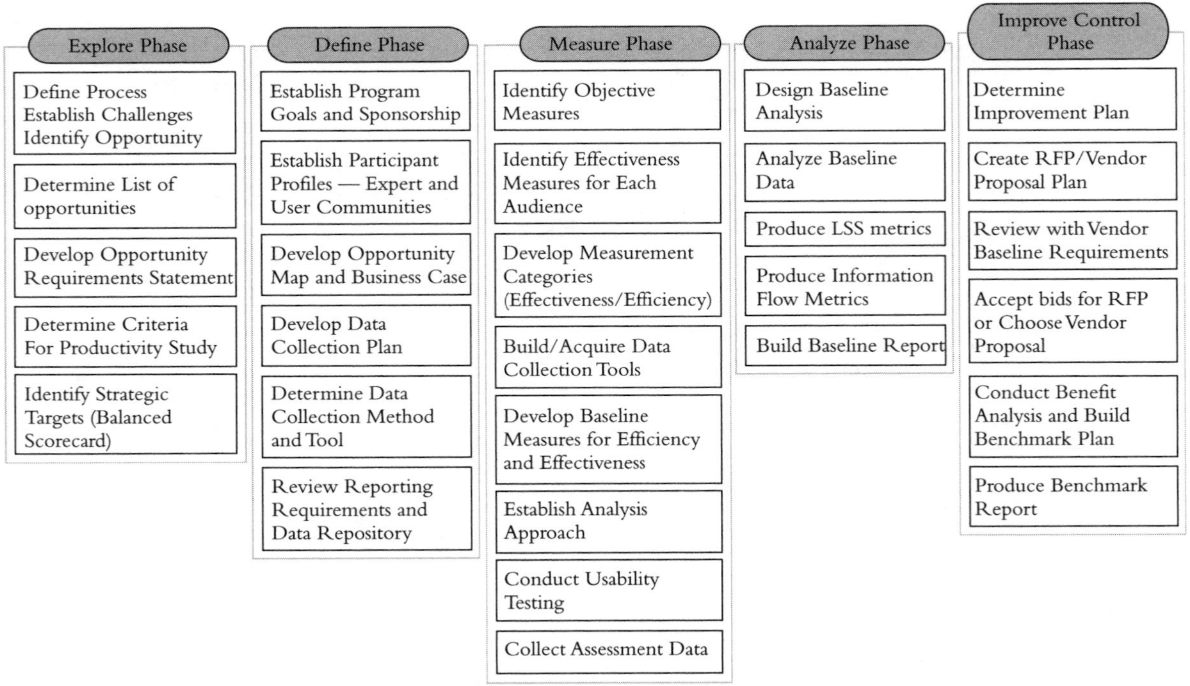

Explore Phase

- Define Process Establish Challenges Identify Opportunity
- Determine List of opportunities
- Develop Opportunity Requirements Statement
- Determine Criteria For Productivity Study
- Identify Strategic Targets (Balanced Scorecard)

Define Phase

- Establish Program Goals and Sponsorship
- Establish Participant Profiles — Expert and User Communities
- Develop Opportunity Map and Business Case
- Develop Data Collection Plan
- Determine Data Collection Method and Tool
- Review Reporting Requirements and Data Repository

Measure Phase

- Identify Objective Measures
- Identify Effectiveness Measures for Each Audience
- Develop Measurement Categories (Effectiveness/Efficiency)
- Build/Acquire Data Collection Tools
- Develop Baseline Measures for Efficiency and Effectiveness
- Establish Analysis Approach
- Conduct Usability Testing
- Collect Assessment Data

Analyze Phase

- Design Baseline Analysis
- Analyze Baseline Data
- Produce LSS metrics
- Produce Information Flow Metrics
- Build Baseline Report

Improve Control Phase

- Determine Improvement Plan
- Create RFP/Vendor Proposal Plan
- Review with Vendor Baseline Requirements
- Accept bids for RFP or Choose Vendor Proposal
- Conduct Benefit Analysis and Build Benchmark Plan
- Produce Benchmark Report

Figure 5.4 Lean Six Sigma—Based PIF Phases

project plan or detailed procedure manual but rather a set of guidelines that should be reflected in a project plan and the detailed documents as the core team builds them. Figure 5.19 at the end of the chapter provides an overview of the entire process.

Explore Phase

The explore phase of the project, as outlined in Figure 5.5, is designed to help the organization define the specific business pain points (or challenges) that require immediate attention and the initial outcomes[1], and outputs that will be measured, as well as target the audience.

A "pain point" represents a business challenge blocking a company from using information to make meaningful, accurate, and timely decisions that increase productivity. It

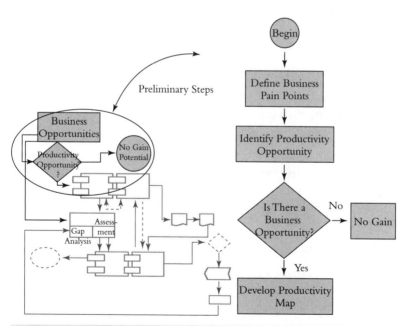

FIGURE 5.5 Explore Phase

could be any point in the organization where a business challenge impacts its performance. The pain point analysis provides a snapshot of the challenges that may be caused by or solved by technology and/or procedure improvements.

Objective of the Explore Phase

Once a business productivity pain point and its targeted opportunity areas are identified, it is relatively easy to target knowledgeable parties for interviews. These interviews can be handled in person and the data collected on spreadsheets or in documents. Alternately, the information can be collected remotely through a web-based (analysis) tool and the results summed up by the core team. Regardless of the approach used to collect the data, a pain point report or list will provide the basis to move forward with a productivity impact study.

The first step is to develop a list of potential opportunities. The example we will use through out this chapter will be from the two case studies described in Chapter 1, the U.S. Air Force and Korean Air, and Case Study 3, the financial institution introduced earlier.

An opportunity summary report, or pain point analysis, of potential improvement opportunities, as shown in Figure 5.6, is designed to present an overview of the business opportunities reviewed in the explore phase. The figure shows the results from the Air Force team during their explore phase. Each opportunity is reviewed for potential productivity gains. A gain can be achieved by changing a business rule, changing a procedure, better utilization of a technology, adding/modifying a technology, or implementing training. Gains can be expressed in terms of effectiveness (improved output/outcomes, customer satisfaction, etc.) or efficiencies (faster processing, lower operating cost, etc.). The core team then ranks and prioritizes opportunities based on greatest impact to the enterprise.

Current Opportunities

☑	Executive Succession Planning and Development (Colonel Management)	✓	Digital Printing and Imaging

Potential Opportunities

	Account Management		Data Migration
	Personnel Retention		E-Mail Retention
	Document Management		Expense Reporting
	Asset Management		Help Desk Self-Servicing
◉	Task Management		Mobile Communications

☑ Completed   ✓ Opportunity Mapped but not assessed   ◉ Target for coming year

FIGURE 5.6 Sample Business Challenges and Related Opportunities

The first step in targeting the business opportunities is to define the pain. Much has been written on defining business pain points or challenges. In general, a business challenge must be discrete and relatively independent of other challenges within the environment. A business pain point maybe defined as:

> A particular ability or capacity that a business requires in order to enable a specific purpose or output—it describes what the business does (outcomes and service levels) that creates value for customers. The definition of the pain point or challenge should include a description of the people, process, technology, information and service-level expectations.

In a PIF program, we seek to measure only the essential performance-related information needed to improve throughput and/or quality delivery.

If the definition of the challenge is not discrete, then management actions in one business challenge will overly affect other business performance within the ecosystem.

A business challenge should be at a high enough level that financial systems can identify its cost data (the input). If resources are shared between challenges, this can be noted and accounted for in the analysis processes.

Second, we need to account for all outputs of the selected business challenge. Outputs can be composed of one or more outcomes. Defining the outputs allows us to judge our ability to develop measures and identify existing metrics for the opportunity.

At the completion of the opportunity exploration, the team delivers a summary report segmenting the opportunities into two categories:

1. Potential for a productivity impact study

2. No potential

For consideration in this program, a business productivity opportunity should address an issue that either will affect a key enterprise deliverable or uses or could use technology. Technology utilization can be as simple as the use of e-mail to transmit information or as complex as changing business rules to employ new technology. To define the opportunities in the Air Force project, the core team identified the target business areas within the agency. Once these were identified, it became clear that there was a potential technology that, if enabled, would improve workflow and there was a metric that could be used to measure the success of the technology implementation.

The opportunities shown in Figure 5.6 were suggested as possible studies areas; they included practices such as human resources (personnel retention) and procurement planning (asset management), and IT(Help Desk Self Servicing). In addition to the participation of the core team in the evaluation process, helpful insights can be gathered from technology vendors with extensive or unique experience in the subject areas, from research studies, and from industry experts. The process of qualifying and prioritizing opportunities can consume a considerable amount of the core team's time. Executive sponsors can help this process along by resolving differences of opinion and providing strategic insight in the prioritization process. After a three-month exploration, our Air Force core team presented current opportunities for a wide spectrum of potential projects, as shown in Figure 5.6. In the end, the chief information officer (the executive sponsor) and his advisory team assisted the core team in the final opportunity section. The opportunities that were not selected for the initial program in Year 1 are listed in Potential Opportunities list and are under consideration in Year 2 of the program.

Even when projects make the initial opportunity list, there may not be a productivity assessment. In the Air Force project, after the initial design stage, the digital print and imaging project was put on hold (as indicated in Figure 5.6). The project team members determined that they could not identify the appropriate sponsor(s), as ownership of the print function (and budget) is different from one facility to another and the budget (against which one would measure the improvement) was not clearly identified for the project. The Year 2 projects include work scenarios such as task management, information request process, and mobile communications. Task management (note the ⊙ symbol indicating a definite project for the next year) and a new–but–associated project, request for information; projects were successfully launched in Year 2. The outcome of this combined investigation is outlined in Case Study 4 in Chapter 6 as we discuss the results of an assessment program.

Define Phase

Output measures (both subjective and objective), as described in Figure 5.7, are developed by completing the opportunity mapping and creating a data collection plan during the define phase of the project. The results of the define phase provide the goals and objectives that are needed to guide the improvement planning process. (See the sections "Analyze Phase" and "Improve/Control Phase" later in the chapter for more detail on improvement planning.)

Objective of the Define Phase
The objective of this phase is to establish an organized set of metrics and measures that track the flow of information and deliverables for the targeted work and roles.

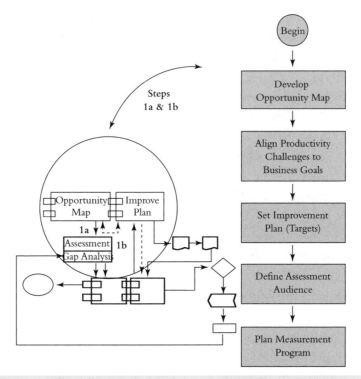

FIGURE 5.7   Define Phase

Recent research demonstrates that the impact of technologies on performance is strongly influenced by the dynamic capabilities of effectiveness (comprising consistency, leverage, alignment, and relevance) and efficiency. The results of the Information Work Productivity Council project mentioned in Chapter 2 noted that work:

> effectiveness (consistency, leverage, alignment and relevance) is an integral and statistically valid measure of the productivity of information work and it explains a significant portion of the variance in firm financial performance. Effectiveness of information work has a significant impact on improvements in firm operating and gross margins, as well as on ROA [return on assets] and EPS [equity per share]. Efficiency of information work has a significant impact only on a single measure of firm performance—ROE [return on equity]. Indeed, our results suggest that prior studies that have attempted to measure the productivity of information work may be inadequate since they only capture the Efficiency dimension of information work. Our results indicate that Effectiveness may be even more important in terms of its impact on several firm financial measures. [2]

Studies such as this one have led to a strong emphasis within the PIF program for a balance between effectiveness and efficiency when planning productivity assessment projects.

Alignment of Outcome Measures to Effectiveness and Efficiency Goals.
The define phase allows us to associate the benefits of efficiency/effectiveness alignment. This approach ties the quantified subjective data to the current capabilities and technology targets and to the activity-based data. This activity-based analysis model provides a unique foundation for each project to correlate the detail measures associated with specific technologies and build a statistical image of information work.

As discussed earlier, many business domains often have multiple outputs. These multiple outputs may be correlated to one another through overlapping outcomes (activities and behaviors that together produce an output). We often see an overlap not only in the visible tasks but in the behaviors and use of enablers (technology, processes, and procedures). A good example of such a complex challenge was Korean Air, where the target audience demonstrated that it had an efficient use of the current technology but that the technology solution was lacking in collaborative features and the workflow suffered from inconsistent process management. In this situation, little would be gained by providing training on the technology itself (attempting to improve efficiency). Here the true opportunity is in the effective integration of existing and improved technology into a streamlined workflow. Establishing a baseline for I-work productivity should also include assessing existing and planned projects (both direct and indirect) that affect the business domain. Figure 5.8 provides a sample of an initial interaction map from the Air Force case studies. This map is interested not for the program names or vendors that are noted on the map but as an example of issues and inter-relationships that must be considered before starting an assessment program. Each potential program and project should be queried for potential impact on the information work measures to ensure the analysis accounts for all known variables.

The example in Figure 5.8 demonstrates a very complex environment that is common in many enterprises today. It is important to understand the enterprise architecture when it comes time to examine improvement options later in the project. At this stage in the project development, this information is used to help ensure all the current technologies are represented in the assessment process (available for the participants to select).

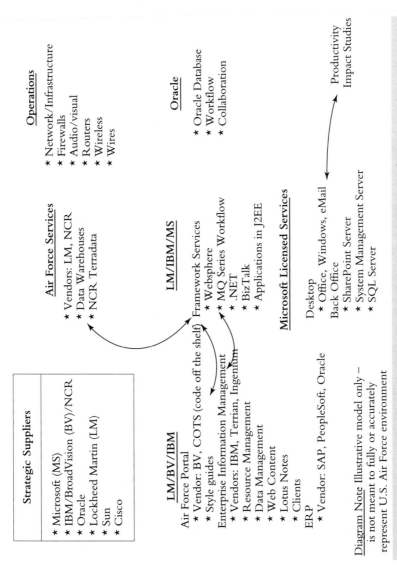

Strategic Suppliers

★ Microsoft (MS)
★ IBM/BroadVision (BV)/NCR
★ Oracle
★ Lockheed Martin (LM)
★ Sun
★ Cisco

LM/BV/IBM

Air Force Portal
★ Vendor: BV, COTS (code off the shelf)
★ Style guides
Enterprise Information Management
★ Vendors: IBM, Terrian, Ingenium
★ Resource Management
★ Data Management
★ Web Content
★ Lotus Notes
★ Clients
ERP
★ Vendor: SAP, PeopleSoft, Oracle

Diagram Note Illustrative model only –
is meant to fully or accurately
represent U.S. Air Force environment

Air Force Services

★ Vendors: LM, NCR
★ Data Warehouses
★ NCR Terradata

LM/IBM/MS

Framework Services
★ Websphere
★ MQ Series Workflow
★ .NET
★ BizTalk
★ Applications in J2EE

Microsoft Licensed Services

Desktop
★ Office, Windows, eMail
Back Office
★ SharePoint Server
★ System Management Server
★ SQL Server

Operations

★ Network/Infrastructure
★ Firewalls
★ Audio/visual
★ Routers
★ Wireless
★ Wires

Oracle

★ Oracle Database
★ Workflow
★ Collaboration

Productivity
Impact Studies

FIGURE 5.8 Sample Programs and Projects Based on U.S. Air Force Study

Building Measures to Capture Efficiency and Effectiveness.
To realize the promise of a productivity impact study, we need to gather working data for a baseline. All productivity models rely on the concept of inputs and outputs that produce value. The measurement of productivity is the relative cost of the deliverable compared to the rate the marketplace would pay, or allocate budget, for it. In other words, we compare the inputs, or resources, to the value of the output. The difficult part of measuring productivity in relation to I-work is that not all work appears to create a measurable output. The *hidden work* of coordinating and handling exceptions is an often-overlooked and undervalued component of the productivity story. Thus, an output (the measurable deliverable) might be composed of a chain of many indirect outcomes (amorphous results). Next we define inputs and outcomes in relation to I-work and describe how to build the measures and metrics to meet the goals set out in your assessment design.

- *Inputs related to outcome/outputs.* Clearly mapping the relationship between inputs (or more simply, resources) and outputs (results/deliverables) is a requirement for any workplace initiative in order to properly judge the proposed productivity gains achieved by an organizational or structural change.
- *Input* is measured as the cost, or the quantifiable effort, to operate a business domain.
- An *outcome, as defined earlier,* is measured in terms of a quantifiable service or product delivered to customers (internal or external) that can be associated with financial metrics.
- *Outputs* are the intermediate view that allows us to group tangible and intangible (I-work) deliverables into "packages" that are recognized as the result of the production work. Often specific outputs are too

"soft" on their own to directly link to financial metrics can be grouped as contributing factors (part of a complex index) to build the actual output that, in turn, is compared to the financial metric. However, in the production model of economics, these outputs may be represented as an aggregate measure of efficiency (e.g. the speed at which the group can produce a document). The PIF model seeks to discover the impact of efficiency and effectiveness (consistency, leverage, alignment, and relevance) on outputs as well as outcomes.

To achieve an improvement goal for a given business opportunity, it is necessary to identify the specific business domain and targets that will be impacted. The isolation of the domain and the deliverables within the domain is critical to ensure an accurate set of measures. If other changes are to, or could potentially, occur in the domain during the measurement period, they must be accounted for if the productivity measure is to be accurate and informative. The same consideration must be given during reassessment periods as well. As shown in Figure 5.9 it is helpful to consider measures in three categories:

- *Managing to long-term results.* Efficiency/effectiveness measures must have the capability to be rolled up to the division level and then across the enterprise in order to provide an indicator of the overall health of I-work productivity. The metrics must have the flexibility to address new questions brought about by changing circumstances. To answer new questions, we must be capable of combining operating measures in new ways and of aggregating or decomposing those measures as necessary. The object-oriented reporting structure (used by tools such as OLAP[3]) of data allows the analysis team to view the productivity improvement (including technology) initiatives in many different ways and to roll-up or drill-down in the structure as necessary.

Performance goals can be stated as either outcomes or outputs (as defined earlier), but to be completed, they should incorporate targets and time frames into a performance measure.

- *Short-term effectiveness performance measures* are the indicators or metrics that are used to gauge program performance. Performance measures can be either outcome or output measures. Using the Air Force example, we might look to improve the team effectiveness in collaboration and communications. In the Korean Air program, one target was *better* decision making. "Better" was defined, in this case, as faster (less wait time by teams waiting for senior management approval). Measuring the behavioral change around collaboration/communication was a matter of recording the changes in the workflow (how work was done from one period to another). Measuring the change in decision making is also a timing issue but requires examining both the outcomes and outputs to determine the changes in the workflow.

- Short-term efficiency targets are the quantifiable or measurable characteristics that tell how well a program must accomplish a performance measure. For example, the targets for the Air Force case study were: (1) reduce data transfer latency, (2) less effort to update candidate list, (3) improve person-to-person–related information delays, and (4) improve candidate management. In the Korean Air case study, the targets were (1) reduce wait time for decisions and (2) improve process cycle efficiency.

In summary, performance goals, as outlined in Figure 5.9, have three components: performance measures, targets, and time frames for realization. For the Air Force case study, the performance goal could be zero overtime by project personnel within two or three complete succession planning cycles. The Korean Air case study might have been to seek an average wait time of no more than 20 minutes by 2008.

PIF measures are gathered at two levels: snapshots and baselines. The initial, or snapshot, assessment collects the views of a limited group of managers and subject matter experts. Productivity Opportunity Mapping (POM) allows the team to probe deeper into the challenges of a work scenario that rated high on the pain point analysis. If the POM analysis provides enough insight to allow the project sponsor to approve a baseline assessment, that in turn helps to establish an improvement plan (as described in Chapters 7 and 8).

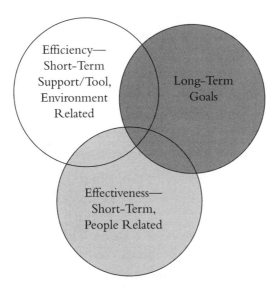

Efficiency—
Short-Term
Support/Tool,
Environment
Related

Long-Term
Goals

Effectiveness—
Short-Term,
People Related

FIGURE 5.9 Targeting Performance Measures

Develop Productivity Opportunity Mapping.
Productivity Opportunity Mapping involves statistically analyzing and mapping multiple procedures across a work scenario. The POM produces a roadmap of the business process, practice, and procedures by establishing a matrix association between the work behaviors, technologies, and deliverables. POM can help managers by providing an opportunity to:

- Define areas of potential productivity improvement
- Identify business issues and technologies with greatest room for improvement
- Help to build organizational agreement for productivity improvement planning, goals, and objectives

A POM can be drawn out in many formats as shown in Figures 5.10 and 5.11. The focal point of a POM, at this point in the PIF process, is to clarify the work scenario in terms of the practices and procedures. The POM further demonstrates some of potential challenges, work behaviors and tools that are currently used in the production of work.

Many organizations prefer customized POMs that demonstrate the subjective management data collected by the core team during the interview process. The Air Force team produced a POM report that initially demonstrated the specific behavioral challenges and the projected areas of improvement without the cause-and-effect diagram shown in Figure 5.10.

The Korean Air team built an initial POM map (Figure 5.11) that emphasized the productivity goals the organization chose during the executive briefing at the outset of the project.

Work Activity	Function	Improvement Opportunity	Target
Content Generation and Management	Profile Building	**Reduce Data Transfer Latency** • Reduce cut-and-paste between data sources and targets • Data search	Reduce % of Time in Data Gathering of Content (Reduce Labor Time)
Information Search and Sharing	List Development	**Less Effort to Update Candidate List** • Increase shared document development through multi-team authoring (must include versioning and automatic data transfer between docs)	Increase % of Work Time Spent in Collaboration (Reduce Document Cycle Time)
Team Collaboration	Document and Information Sharing	**Improve Person-to-Person-Related Information Delays** • Provide procedures for electronic sharing • Increase (leverage) use of shared electronic space for information exchange	Reduce % of Rework and Increase Quality Output for Content (Reduce Labor Hours over All Cycle Time)
Communications	Candidate Visibility	**Improve Candidate Management** • Leverage electronic connectivity notification and training for decision makers in the placement and advancement of candidates	Reduce % of Time in Communication (Improve Overall Delivery Time and Quality)

Opportunity: Candidate Information Flow

FIGURE 5.10 U.S. Air Force Sample POM Report

Organizational Goal: Productivity Enhancement and Cost Avoidance

Improvement Opportunities	Target's Departments	Improvement Impact $ in Millions
Reduce Data Transfer Latency • Reduce cut-and-paste between data sources & targets • Data search	Sales HR IT	Cost Avoidance
Less Effort to Update Documentation • Increase shared document development through multi-team authoring (including versioning and automatic data transfer between documents)	Sales Strategy HR	
Improve Person-to-Person–Related Information Delays Provide procedures for electronic sharing • Increase (leverage) use of shared electronic space for information exchange	Purchasing Strategy Maintenance IT General Affairs	Revenue Enhancement
Less Effort to Receive Approvals • Leverage electronic connectivity notification and training for decision makers	Strategy Call Center	

Opportunity: Information Distribution

Efficiency Gain from: Search and Retrieval and Content Generation
- Trend Building
- Document Development

Improve Effectiveness through: Team Collaboration and Communications
- Document and Information Sharing
- Notifications

FIGURE 5.11 Korean Air Sample POM Report

Regardless of the shape or orientation, the POM is a strong visual image that helps core team members demonstrate the challenges they are seeing within the target work scenario. The initial POM helps program managers determine if the work scenario warrants a deeper baseline assessment.

Develop Data Collection Plan (Methods and Tools).
The baseline assessment is used to provide broad productivity analysis data on key organizational business challenges identified through pain point analysis and POM processes. Data collected in the measure phase of the PIF process provides a view into the technology utilization and information complexity that can affect organizational productivity at the process, practice, and procedure level. A baseline assessment helps managers by creating the foundation for a gap analysis and measurement report by detailing the impact of technology and procedures on the target work area. This pivotal step in the PIF process enables a business leader to analyze and measure business challenges, current technologies deployed, and what technologies are needed to solve business challenges and increase productivity.

Defining the overall PIF project is the turning point in the process. The POM adds depth to the definition phase that is often missing in purely subjective processes. Allowing operational managers and subject matter experts to participate in this initial opportunity analysis provides the project sponsor with a broader vision and acceptance of the productivity impact analysis and, ultimately, the improvement plan.

Measure Phase

During the measure phase, we identify and collect subjective and objective assessment data. We also obtain financial

(cost) data to establish input (objective) measures and baseline for metrics

Objective of the Measure Phase.
The objective of this phase is to collect complete, relevant,
and timely data.

As demonstrated by the breakout diagram in Figure 5.12,
the goal of the measure phase is to reduce the complexity
and difficulty of the assessment instruments and collect the
required data. This activity results in lower frustration and less
confusion by participants; the more frustrated and confused
your participants are, the more your results will be compro-
mised. To complete the measure phase, the core team establishes the measures to be used, agrees on a data collection

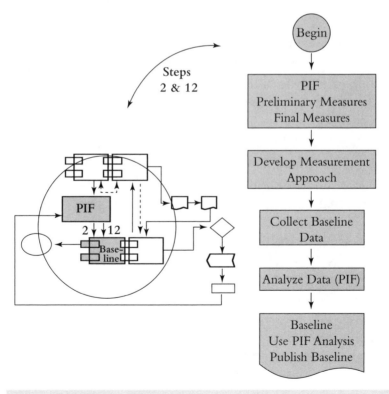

FIGURE 5.12 Measure Phase

scheme, collects data, and completes the preliminary analysis of the results.

Among the tasks to be completed in the measure phase are the customization of data collection tools and content and the request for and collection of data. To accomplish this goal, the team may review demographic or geographic information that is essential and invaluable for interpreting the results of the project. As you know, PIF is built on the concept that there are five key behaviors practiced by all information workers:

- Content generation and management
- Asynchronous communication
- Synchronous communication (collaboration)
- Search and retrieval (research)
- Problem solving and analysis

It is the unique intersection of these behaviors and the technology and the work to be achieved that produces a truly productive procedure. Customizing the procedure list used in the assessment will increase the quality of the data collection by clarifying the intent or target of the assessment.

A reminder note on choosing the assessment target: When determining the work scenario to assess, it is important to keep the target opportunity in mind. The chosen assessment target, within the business domain (or process area), is the definable intersection of the process (business rules), the current practices (work behaviors), and the technology enablers, as illustrated in Figure 5.13. Within this carefully defined zone, the assessment program should establish a consistent baseline. A well-developed baseline can potentially account for the wide range of drivers and participants (agents) that impact information-centric productivity. This view should allow those working within the environment and those seeking to manage and support the environment to understand and participate equally in improvement goals. It is at this intersection that PIF can provide a foundation for a standardized measurement approach to productivity improvement.

Obtain Financial (Cost) Data to Establish a Composite Input (Objective) Measure.

As mentioned earlier, the financial/cost data should represent all of the resources working on the identified outcomes within the business domain.[4] The data should reflect the actual cost of providing all of the products and services to internal/external customers/vendors of the business domain. *One key to determining productivity gains is to be consistent.* In most cases, the goal is to determine the magnitude of the improvement possible and trend the gains over time. If the organization desires to cut costs through productivity improvements, obtaining and measuring input cost by dollar amounts (rather than percentage estimates) is more critical than if the organization desires to improve service (at the same or improved level of cost). As discussed earlier with regard to outcomes, it may not always be possible or desirable to provide full cost data in some

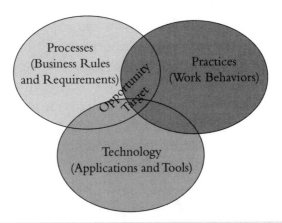

FIGURE 5.13 Assessment Targeting

non-industrial business domains (e.g., acquisition or logistics) where reporting systems may track only salary costs. Salary costs usually represent the majority of the costs in these areas. Other costs (e.g., supplies and office space) in these areas are generally allocated as a percent of salaries or on a head-count basis. In such cases, the estimated cost data (by percent) may be added to the known costs programmatically for the development of the productivity trends. In more industrial settings (e.g., maintenance), where wages are just one element (and often a much smaller proportion) of the costs, reporting systems usually reflect manpower, materials, and equipment in cost data. For this reason, costs reported for industrial work scenarios are normally more precise and appear easier to obtain.

For the cost data, you will have to match the frequency and length of the output data. If you use quarterly data over five years (20 observable periods) for the output data, you will need to obtain quarterly cost data over the same five years. This will permit a valid cost–output data analysis.

To develop a productivity trend, you might want to review the actual cost of operating the defined business opportunity to develop a realistic trend. When developing the predictive model of productivity benefit, you will also need to adjust for inflation. Using the appropriate index of the Bureau of Labor Statistics is one way to do this.[5] As with the composite output index, you might find it useful to use the last quarter in the five-year history of costs as the base period for adjusting for inflation of costs.

Creating Data Collection Tools.
In the name of efficiency and consistency, the core team should review and suggest modifications to any standardized tool to fit the culture and voice of the enterprise. Tools such as those provided by professional assessment organizations (e.g., those found at *www.productivityexchange.org*) are designed to be used by all organizations with minimal modifications.

These tools are created through research to measure the information workflow in a number of commercial and public settings and will require only minor editing and alignment before use within your enterprise.

Tasks Associated with Survey Revision and Data Collection.
For detailed or specific task lists and relative timing, your team will need to build a three-step project-specific plan.

1. Review and make change requests for initial testing at workshops (with managers and I-workers from the target work scenario).

    a. Evaluate current version of the assessment tools (surveys) based on business challenge/domain, targeted roles, and measures to be collected.

    b. Assess papers and published materials related to the target work and deliverables.

    c. Interview contacts (whose names and contact information will be supplied by your organization as the communication focal point) to understand their goals and objectives.

    d. Incorporate findings from a, b, and c in a request form to vendor.

    e. Confer with the larger team and program sponsor via conference call to discuss any program revisions.

    f. Establish a testing process.

2. Optional: Site interviews and workshops.

    a. Analyze and write up observations from the testing process.

    b. Confer with business owners about general findings and conclusions from each workshop.

   c. After-site data collection: Incorporate findings in a revised change request for further discussion with the vendor (if using an outside agency for data collection).

  3. Update, or request vendor to update, the data collection tool (survey) based on tasks 1 and 2.

Collect Subjective and Objective Data.
Subjective Data Collection
Establish the audience size for both the top-down (manager view) and bottom-up (I-worker view) within the target work scenario. In general, an assessment audience of 20 to 40 percent of the target work scenario audience (depending on the size of the group) is statistically sound. This data will help to support or modify the conclusions built by the core team during the exploration and design phases of the project.

The PIF measurement structure will help to convert program objectives into effectiveness and efficiency targets. As outlined in Figure 5.14, objectives are first divided into tangible and intangible categories then broken down into logical components (or objects such as tangible assets–printers or intangible assets—task tracking). The components are in turn described by their attributes (e.g., model or speed) or behavior (e.g., work type, e.g. collaboration) or technology used (e.g. word processing). Attributes can in turn be quantified and analyzed. The program not only measures the visible attributes but views the impact of intangible components, such as service and availability, on I-Work productivity (which can be expressed in labor dollars).

Financial/Output Metrics Data Collection
The data collection for objective financial metrics is based on the opportunities chosen during the explore phase and outlined during the actual design phases of the project.

Tangible		
Measures		**Metrics**
Profile	Model Number	Cost Output Service Level Efficiency Rating
	Serial Number	
	Purchase Date	
	Life	
Attributes	Speed	
	Supply Requirements	
	Feature	
Detail	Unique Features	
	Finish	
	Color	
Intangible		
Measures		**Metrics**
Profile	Work Type	Effectiveness Efficiency Complexity Interdependencies Usage Output
	Work Location	
	Work Complexity	
Attributes	Technology Used	
	Application Procedures	
	Skill Level	
Detail	Utilization Pattern	
	Cycle Time	

FIGURE 5.14 Measurement Structure

Output metrics should be related back to standard organizational metrics or key performance indicators (KPIs). Since the major cost in the think factory is labor, most cost-reduction KPIs include reducing the cost of labor. Streamlining the work scenario is one of the best ways to improve cost performance. Work scenario streamlining can help the team set the reduction target, as in the case of the Air Force (Figure 5.16), where we set a target of reducing the process cycle time required to complete the work scenario by 5 percent. Although it was important to the Air Force team to cut the amount of overtime currently required to accomplish the work, it was equally, if not more, important to find the time to invest in quality improvement. The labor reduction was potentially worth over $1 million to the organizational budget; improving the quality of the selection process is an undetermined financial but highly valued benefit.

So-called soft benefits are not always easy to explain and are even harder to detail, especially when they do not involve a reduction in force. In the Air Force study, the goal that was reviewed was to reduce the level of personnel required to accomplish a task, allowing more experienced senior personnel to focus on quality improvements. Reducing the skill level required to accomplish a work scenario by institutionalizing the existing knowledge in newly streamlined procedures is one way to accomplish a cost savings while ensuring the continuity of the business.

Business Benefits	YR 0 ($)	YR 1 ($)	YR 2 ($)	YR 3 ($)
Succession Planning	157,252	157,152	432,369	432,369
Game Planning: Reduced Exceptions (Improved Workflow)	5,000	5,000	10,000	10,000
Game Planning: Improve Collaboration (Decrease Meetings 1/week)	12,639	12,639	25,278	25,278
Reduced/streamlined collaboration (Move from E-Mail)	34,452	34,352	51,628	51,628
Improved Information Search	150,161	150,161	157,741	157,741
Reduced Skill Level Demand	—	—	187,722	187,722

FIGURE 5.15 Air Force Case Study: Potential Financial Benefit

Baseline Assessments Frequently Asked Questions

Before launching an assessment process, reviewing and rewriting the FAQs that follow based on the culture and structure of your organization may be helpful. .

Q1. Who should run the assessments?
A. The organization directly impacted by the improvement, with the assistance of a third-party consultant, should develop its own baselines and benchmarks.

Q2. How are assessments funded?
A. Benchmarking should be paid for by the impacted organization as a service separate and apart from the improvement projects that are recommended to fill gaps in performance.

Q3. How do you make sure the assessments are relevant?
A. The core team should work with each group seeking productivity assessment programs to align relevant measurement objects and to generally make sure the project is relevant and useful to the stated goals of the group.

Q4. What is the role of the core team?
A. The role of the core team is to guide the design of the benchmark, associate the right data-gathering template, help develop appropriate key performance indicators (KPIs), and make sure the project will be aligned to the group's primary mission.

Q5. What measures are reported?
A. The actual measures vary according to the subject matter, but they generally include:

- *Financial,* such as cost per unit of service delivered
- *Service,* such as percentage of service delivered within service standards

- *Internal performance,* such as average number of employees required to deliver a unit of service
- *People management,* such as end user impact (if you remove printers) or training (if administrative staff must be trained to replace ink cartridges)
- *Site and group profile,* includes more qualitative questions designed to collect information about current work processes and practices.

Q6. Who owns the data that is gathered during the course of an assessment exercise, and what happens to it afterward?
A. Data supplied to the project by participants should always remain the intellectual property of the sponsoring organization. The organization must store and secure this data. *Note:* The sponsoring organization must provide security requirements for data prior to the start of the project.

Q7. Will my data be identifiable?
A. The benchmark methodology does not allow any individual participant to be identified. This is achieved by the use of derived data (e.g., ratios and percentages) rather than raw data and by the use of identification codes. When the data analysis is provided by a third-party vendor supporting the assessment, the analysis methods are the intellectual property of the vendor. The data and results, however, should remain the property of the sponsoring organization. If data is used as part of a reference database that is used to drive industry benchmarks, the vendor should provide safeguards to ensure that no search will reveal the identity of a specific individual (if you have chosen to reveal your participation at a detail level) or company (at a summary level) without permission.

Q8. We're busy. How much staff time will be involved to provide data?
A. The data-gathering process has been designed to be as minimally intrusive as possible. There may be a need for

some internal coordination to collect data from all the relevant areas of your group. Every project should have a project manager for this purpose. The involvement is approximately 8 to 20 hours/week (depending on the size of your project) for the duration of the project for this task (average PIF projects run two to four weeks, but large projects could run several months.

Some numbers will be required (from your budget, assets, personnel, etc.) so that performance can be compared against identified key performance indicators, but most of this should already be available from your budget and reports you produce for other purposes. The KPIs for each assessment are developed in collaboration with the appropriate subject matter experts and take into consideration the data available to the group. Some teams (e.g., the financial services team in Case Study 3) struggle with this concept as they work on appropriate data if, for example, there is no consistent or official output for a suggested procedure. In general, the teams work around these issues by using industry-standard input to help participants agree on work scenario content.

A week is generally recommended for online data gathering and entry (on average projects). If you can preset much of the user profile information before the assessment starts it will probably take your group less than a week to complete the online questionnaire. Always set a specific window of time for data collection. Announce the start and stop dates and time (e.g. close of business) in the same e-mail or memo used to invite people to participate.

To many, the measurement phase seems like the central or focal point of the PIF process. Although it is the part of the program that directly touches the greatest number of people, it should not be seen as the essence of the program. Collecting data is important, but collecting the right data and properly analyzing that data is even more important. The design and analyze phases of the program are more central to development productivity than the number of people assessed.

Analyze Phase

The analyze phase focuses on reviewing, collating and surfacing the results of the data collection process. The analysis approach will have been established by the core team during the design phase. There are two facets of analysis: building the baseline, or AS IS, report and comparing output measures to help the team Implementation Plans (or TO BE goals based on the gap analysis).

Objective of Analyze Phase: Baseline Reporting.
During this phase, you analyze inputs (cost and financial) and outcomes measures aggregated to output metrics and produce productivity baseline reports (the AS-IS state) as described in Figure 5.16.

Analyze Input (Financial) and Output Measures.
To create a productivity baseline report, we need to align the subjective and objective data sets collected during the assessment phase. The goal of the data alignment and analysis is to create a set of quantitative metric of I-work (activity) against each output that is easy to understand. The improvement plan, initiated during the define phase, is completed during the analyze phase. The information derived from this analysis allows the team to build out the requirements for the change plan that forms the project

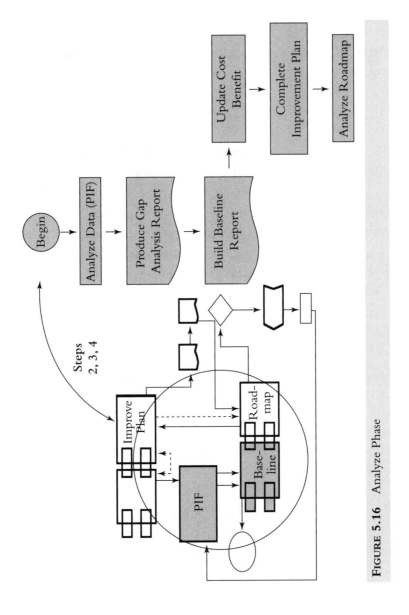

Figure 5.16 Analyze Phase

improvement roadmap. The project roadmap is an action plan for collecting and analyzing internal and external improvement recommendations (proposals). The analyze phase is focused on both reviewing the results of the assessment gap analysis and planning for the way forward.

Implementing Productivity Plans.
Once the data analysis is complete, we will again view all opportunities. The sponsor or management team will decide, on the strength of the data presented and the ranking of the opportunities (greatest to least potential), the improvement plans they want to move forward with in the near future.

To develop the Air Force plan, the core team participated in an Architectural Design Session (ADS) with Microsoft Consulting Services. The two-day session, held in August 2005, identified quick wins that could increase productivity in the short term without a dramatic increase in technology investment for the agency. The team also sought to envision what the process may evolve into in the future as the agency deploys new technologies. The selection process portion of the work scenario was identified as the short-term improvement area, leveraging the use of Microsoft collaboration and document-sharing technologies. A detailed project plan was created to show the timeline, resources, and cost estimates to implement phase one of the improvement roadmap for management to review.

Improve/Control Phase

The improve and control phase, described in Figure 5.17, of the project starts when the analysis is completed and improvement plans can be established against agreed upon

KPIs. The control aspect of the project includes any bench-mark assessment the business agrees to as part of the overall measurement plan. Most organizations will want to establish a minimum of at least one checkpoint after the improvements are instituted.

Objective of the Improve Phase.
The objective of the improve phase is benchmarking (reassessment over time) or the establishment of a trend line to help management approve improvement plans.

Trend and Analyze Input (Financial) and Output Measures.
To produce a productivity trend, we align the outcome(s)—(subjective and objective data aligned to the effectiveness/efficiency goals)—to the outputs (measurable deliverables) and to the financial data by formula.

Various cost-output relationships can be explored. Numerous statistical analysis programs can be used for this purpose. Generally our academic associates use SPSS Inc. statistical analysis software to develop the models; however, other personal computer statistical packages may also be acceptable.

To provide a realistic picture of potential productivity gains, the projected improvement trends will need to reflect inflation as a dependent variable and the composite output index as the independent variable. The trend analysis should also test for possible differences in the constants with quarterly returns (taking into account cyclical or exceptional activities) by inserting dummy (stand-in) variables to account for unusual costs. Also, if there are several units within the business domain, we will want to pool those data and statistically test for possible differences in

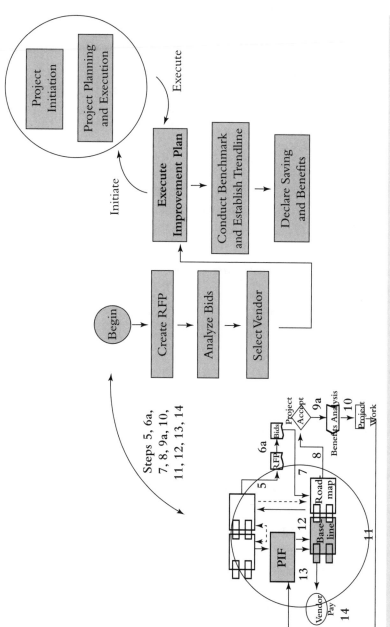

FIGURE 5.17 Improve/Control Phase

119

output slopes or constants, depending on those units. Doing this will let you set trend lines to compare business units within the same organization (internal benchmarking) or against similar business units within the same business sector (industry benchmarking).

Initially you may want to view a simple linear trend demonstrating inputs/outputs for each target business opportunity. This trend analysis should offer the most flexible set of views to the enterprise. It implies a nonlinear view as well as a comparative vision site by site. These views allow you to look at the business challenges over time and by unit. This trending can show multiple results, depending on the particular experience, and accounts for culture, structure, and other situational differences. Based on these trend lines, projections can be developed for future programs (change) and the measures used as the baseline for assessing future improvements.

Repeating Productivity Assessments for Trending.
The measures and metrics must be repeatable from period to period for analysis that will lead to the development of productivity trends. Thus, it will be critical to establish, for each business domain, consistent and reliable data points to compose the input and outcome indices. Input and/or outcome exceptions will need to be dealt with during the construction of the indexes. Exceptions often consume more resources and hinder outcomes to a greater degree than normal processing. These abnormalities should be identified during the baselining process, and recommendations for managing them should be included in the improvement plan. Handling requests as exceptions to the established procedures represents a potential change in the business. Exceptions, such as rework, represent variance

in the workflow and challenges to productivity. Productivity trends are discussed later in the proposal; note that these trends provide the basis for iterative improvement planning.

Validating Measures and Metrics.
The measures and metrics must be capable of verification in terms of how well a change in the input/cost (resources, dollars, and/or quality) of production is reflected in the change in the output. Using this approach, the core team's productivity opportunity hypothesis (established in the explore and define phases of the project) is validated with subjective surveys and repeatable measurement components of the behaviors/activities through both survey and on-site quantitative evaluations. The ability to demonstrate the change in the metric is essential in providing management with a sense of how well an improvement plan is working. All data collection should be validated by a statistically significant audience sampling (20 to 40 percent of the target audience is recommended).

Using Existing Measures.
To the extent possible, each participating business unit should take advantage of existing data collection systems to accumulate input costs/resources and outputs. New metrics should be instituted only when existing metrics and data collection methods are insufficient or nonexistent.

Objective of the Control Phase.
The objective here is the benchmark results analysis, which develops the risk assessment for each improvement proposal and validates the measures/metrics for approved plans over time.

Interpret Productivity Results.

There are four concepts to keep in mind when interpreting the results of the productivity trends and their implications:

1. View efficiency based on the profile results. The analysis team can look at the business domain's optimal point of operation (based on given characteristics). Utilizing a set of "dummy variables," the team can examine different operating parameters based on configuration or characterize an operation as above/below a baseline (once the baseline is established).

2. Focus on whether recent operations are improving by moving closer to the optimal productivity (efficiency/effectiveness) point. Plotting the trend line and annotating it with the last few periods is useful for this purpose. It will allow you to say whether the current workload is typical, declining, or increasing. It also will allow you to say whether the productivity is stagnating, improving, or declining (in reference to the baseline period).

3. Use the trend lines to evaluate future process improvements. Successful process improvements should result in an improved productivity curve. You can develop a statistical test to demonstrate whether the improvement plan will result in a shift up or down.

4. Use the productivity trend as a tool to track progress on improvement plans (assuming given processes hold).

Chapter 3 outlined the three levels of analysis used in PIF: Sigma level, delivery velocity, and information flow indicators. Sigma level and delivery velocity are designed as high-level indicators of process/practice health. The information flow indicators represent the baseline measures that point to improvement opportunities. These indicators plus other efficiency and effectiveness measures unique to your organization should follow solid analysis methodology and above all be repeatable to enable you to develop a trend line.

PIF PLAN SUMMARY

The workflow diagram shown in Figure 5.18 summarizes the Lean Six Sigma–PIF impact study plan. Unlike the earlier Measurement Roadmap this outline demonstrates the process from the initial Explore phase (identifying the business domain/opportunities) through results analysis and improvement planning.

CONCLUSION

The PIF approach examines the reach and quantifies the impact of business procedures and technology utilization on the ability of the process to deliver required outputs. Rather than just focus on the output metrics PIF analyzes the behaviors and the tools used in the course of doing business. PIF builds the statistical sign posts that guide business leaders in planning future improvements and establishes the baseline against which to benchmark improvement.

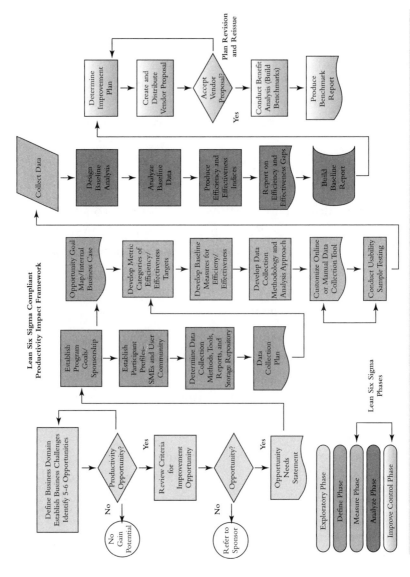

FIGURE 5.18 Lean Six Sigma–PIF Impact Study Plan Summary

124

ENDNOTES

1. Outcomes (or interium deliverables) are a set of activities and behaviors that result in a measurable output (final deliverables).

2. Vish Krishnan, IWPC white paper, 2004.

3. OLAP is an acronym for "On Line Analytical Processing." It is an approach to quickly provide the answer to analytical queries that are dimensional in nature.

4. Dividing resource cost: Make sure you identify *all* the expenses of the business opportunity first and then isolate those associated with the target outputs. Some costs will require allocation across more than one output. If the resource is consumed 100 percent in the course of outputs associated with a single outcome, you do not need to worry about the split. Some business opportunities may not track cost data for each output. If that is the case, we recommend using the statistical technique of principal component analysis as an alternative. Principal component analysis automatically creates the standard normal variables, assigning fixed weights in such a way that inherent variances of the individual measures are reflected as much as possible in the composite output measure.

5. The Department of Defense comptroller inflation data are provided annually only and are not useful to adjust for quarterly inflation.

∞6∞

Measure to Improve,
Not to Manage

Enterprise investment in technology, training, or procedure improvements must be focused on upgrading the ability of the workforce to deliver on the business mission. Deepening the quality of labor (its capability and its ability to work) ultimately improves this performance. Establishing a baseline and periodic measurement only indicates what a program should be accomplishing and whether results have been achieved. Measures help managers by providing information on how future resources and efforts should be allocated to ensure effectiveness. Used correctly, measures can keep program or technology partners focused on the key goals of a program. Correctly targeted technology can enhance delivery.

RIGHT ANSWER—WRONG QUESTION

The wrong technology, no matter how exciting or innovative, can actually reduce or hinder productivity. Three years ago, I watched a major pharmaceutical company struggle with the business value of a new instant messaging application. Initially, the information technology (IT) department thought this new capability would help to

126

improve workflow issues in market research. Unfortunately, the department did not assess the work environment or adequately address the regulatory requirements surrounding the tasks facing the market research teams. The technology was introduced and training was made available to the research teams. After a few weeks, it became obvious that the team managers and researchers were not embracing the new technology. Until the IT department addressed the unique challenges of the researchers, the investment remained underutilized, representing a creditability challenge for the IT department. Using a well-articulated perfor-mance assessment can help in avoiding these challenges by targeting the investment and providing justification for budget proposals by indicating how all stakeholders (stockholders, taxpayers, and others) will benefit.

PERFORMANCE MANAGEMENT AND PRODUCTIVITY MEASUREMENT

Performance measurement data, produced by a productivity assessment, is just part of the information package that managers and policy officials need to make decisions. Good improvement plans are a result of holistic thinking that focuses on performance management, governance, and continuous improvement. An enterprise needs more than a technology architecture to achieve these goals; it needs a business architecture that aligns the work behaviors to the deliverables. To put it simply, to build a solid performance management program, an organization needs more than just a baseline measure.

Building a holistic productivity improvement plan involves both pre- and post assessment work. Performance measurement needs to be coupled with an analysis of the procedures within the work scenario, the risk of not delivering the outputs and outcomes of the work, and the value of the work (to the enterprise and/or customers). This combined set of information allows you to increase your understanding of why results occur and what value an improvement program adds to the enterprise. Improving an outdated or marginally useful work scenario institutionalizes waste. Improving the workflow that supports filing paperwork may appear to drive up productivity unless the paperwork being filed is generated from electronic files. This odd circumstance was outlined during a conversation with military officers last year. Paperwork management was high on their list of improvement productivity projects. A short value stream analysis revealed that most of the paperwork being managed was received as electronic files, which were then printed out and filed in secure cabinets—all according to proper procedure. Streamlining this process would promote and facilitate outdated procedures. A number of years ago I did a study on a warehouse system for a major petrochemicals company. The company management thought the inventory system was outdated and needed to be replaced because the reports did not tally with spot checks of the inventory. The technology department declared that the five-year-old system needed to be replaced, but a performance assessment revealed that site personnel had not been fully trained in the system. The lack of training and outdated procedures were the underlying root causes of the failure. If training and procedure streamlining had not been included in the improvement plan, the business would have continued to suffer from information flow challenges. In other words, performance measurement cannot replace information on the work scenario, costs factors, political judgments about priorities, creativity about solutions, or plain old common sense.

In this chapter we discuss the Productivity Impact Framework (PIF) approach to productivity improvement projects. Our primary reference will be a second U.S. Air Force project, Case Study 4.

CASE STUDY 4: U.S. AIR FORCE: GETTING AND GIVING INFORMATION

In the military, one of the primary requirements is the ability to communicate requests and receive prompt, complete, and accurate answers. A project team was tasked by leadership of a major U.S. Air Force base to improve their request for information (RFI) and task management processes. The challenge faced at this base is typical of many growing enterprises. As a result of regional consolidations and increased global activities the base population, responsibilities and facilities are growing rapidly. The informal workflow for requesting both routine and classified information and task management were failing to meet the demands of the increased population. In the case of an RFI, the information broker (person receiving the initial request) often found it necessary to rework (shape) the request in order to gather the data from the source. As demonstrated in Figure 6.1, the hidden factory map reveals that task management personnel found themselves in a similar dilemma: restructuring orders before they could be resourced and distributed to the people who would execute them. The goal set by the core team was to streamline the procedures (where possible) by introducing new facilitating technology, as shown on the right-hand side of the figure.

Building a model of the hidden factory supporting each work scenario allows the core team and the sponsors to visualize the challenges (the barriers to the information flow) and identify the major required procedures in both work scenarios. Using preliminary Productivity Opportunity Mapping (POM) the task management/RFI core team was also able to strategize with the program sponsor and work group leaders what the future might look like while the productivity data was collected across the organization. This program has completed the baseline study and is planning a benchmark assessment within four weeks of completing the development and execution of an improvement roadmap. Although initially the work scenarios seemed very different, the top-down interviews and assessments demonstrated a

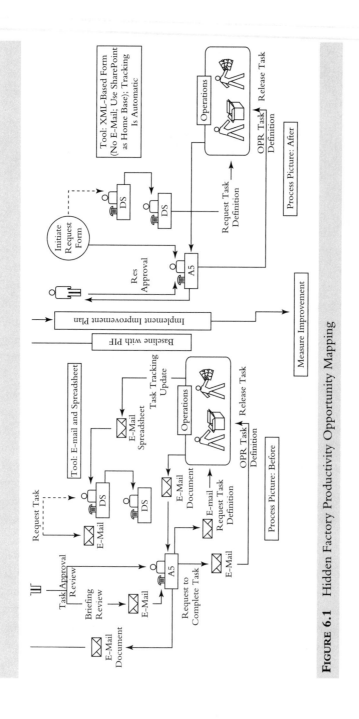

FIGURE 6.1 Hidden Factory Productivity Opportunity Mapping

common set of core procedures. The work behaviors and information flows proved different, as one would expect. In addition, there are different executing roles, but often the same set of initiators exists for both work scenarios. An initial top-down assessment was conducted and clearly identified challenges for both work scenarios in:

* ❖ Data clarity and consistency
* ❖ Notification and information acquisition

In the majority of cases, the information provided to initiate the work scenario suffers from a lack of structure, leading to miscommunications and rework. As the command grows in size, these productivity issues are becoming more challenging.

In both work scenarios, the data and the subject matter expert (SME) interviews exposed major workflow challenges in the work scenario start-up phase as well as increasing challenges in the request closure phase of the workflow. The complete turnaround on this project was estimated to be eight weeks. Quick feedback on improvements is important to allow for quick course correction and participant recognition. The feedback and closure loop is critical to setting the stage for future improvements. We will use the data from this study, as well as some the case studies introduced earlier, to explore productivity assessment measures.

THE SIGMA IN I-WORK

Delivering high-quality, cost-effective products and services is the ultimate goal of most businesses. The implication of a Lean Six Sigma (LSS)–compliant program goes beyond just an indication of quality delivery or customer satisfaction.

The objective of an LSS program is to reduce process output variation over the long term, which Motorola and others have found is directly related to customer experience over time.

LSS focuses PIF reporting on process/procedure effectiveness (capability) and efficiency (ease or speed of delivery). The measurement goal is to determine the sources of variation and time bottlenecks. PIF results are reported through three meters, as shown in Figure 6.2: the Sigma, delivery velocity, and information flow indexes.

Sigma Indicator

The Sigma indicator provides a view of process/practice measured on a Sigma scale against the standard deviation of

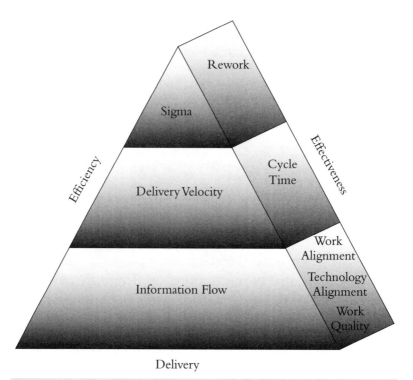

FIGURE 6.2 Productivity Impact Measurement Structure

target audience responses regarding rework (of target deliverables), effectiveness (of technology), and quality (from work behaviors).

Process and practice views are built based only on the procedures in the work scenario. It is often difficult to judge an entire process or even a practice (functional) area within an organization until the majority of the work scenarios within those areas have been assessed. These views may be interesting but must be considered incomplete until a significant number of work scenarios within the process/practice domain have been analyzed.

Once the top-down (desired state) and bottom-up assessments (baseline of the current state) are complete, the Sigma indicator demonstrates the gap between the manager view and the information worker (I-worker) view.

The Sigma of the answers gives an indication the relative health of the work scenario. Case Study 4, from the U.S. Air Force examined two work scenarios in the same process area—Task Management and Request for Information—both work scenarios demonstrated low Sigma levels, as shown in Figure 6.3. The Sigma level indicated that more than 70% of the work within both work scenarios required clarification or rework. The gap, shown in the last column of Figure 6.3, between the current level and the desired level of

Process/ Practice	Desired Sigma Level Indicator (POM)	Current Sigma Level Indicator (PBA)	Sigma Gap
Task Management	3	2.1	0.9
Request for Information	3	2.6	0.4

FIGURE 6.3 Sigma Indicators for Two Process Areas in Case Study 4

operation was significant enough to warrant an examination of the Delivery Velocity and Process Cycle Efficiency.

Delivery is the core of procedure-based work scenarios. In information work (I-Work), the root cause failure is rework and seen in excessive cycle time (the section "Delivery Velocity" provides more detail on cycle time issues). Deliverable rework (one of three elements measured) may be as complex as a contract or engineering schematic or as simple as a phone call. There are numerous ways to improve a situation depending on the type of deliverable, the work behaviors required, and the tools available. The gap report indicates what to fix, not how to fix it.

The Sigma level is the first indicator of process/practice health. If the Sigma level indicator is unacceptable or the gap too large, the next meter to view is the delivery velocity.

Delivery Velocity Meter

The delivery velocity meter provides a view of the time to delivered units/time (cycle time focus). The meter at the practice (function) level provides an average velocity of the deliverables for the practice. If it is unacceptable or requires

Process/ Practice	Desired Delivery Velocity (POM)	Current Delivery Velocity (PBA)	Velocity Gap
Task Management	1/Hour	.64/Hour	.36/Hour
Request for Information	2/Week	.72/Week	1.28/Week

FIGURE 6.4 Delivery Velocity Indicator with Two Process Areas Shown in Case Study 4

Define— Administrative Tasks:	0.05 Tasks Defined/Hr
Define— Operational Tasks:	0.01 Tasks Defined/Hr
Issue:	1.25 Tasks Issued/Hr
Tracked:	0.06 Tasks Tracked/Hr
Recorded:	1.25 Tasks Recorded/Hr

FIGURE 6.5 Task Management Deliverable Velocity Scores in Case Study 4

further investigation, then the average velocity by procedure should be viewed. The same analysis methodology is used to investigate deliverables at the procedure level.

The gap between manager view (Desired Delivery Velocity) and I-worker view (Current Delivery Velocity) when both top-down (POM) and bottom-up (productivity baseline assessment [PBA]) are completed is demonstrated in Figure 6.4.

The meter can be run at both the process level, practice (functional) level, as shown in Figure 6.4 and at the procedure level, as shown in Figure 6.5. Drilling down into the Delivery Velocity allows the project team to pin point the area of the work scenario that is impacting productivity. If Delivery Velocity is poor the work scenario is generally considered to have poor effectiveness rating (low customer satisfaction).

To increase velocity, you need to eliminate waste (time traps) or non-value-added procedures. Wasted time (in a process) is generally associated with rework or wait time. I-work deliverables are often caught in either an analysis or an approval time trap. By applying the 80/20 rule to this paradox, it is relatively safe to say that 80 percent of the time spent in non-optimized procedures is a result of waiting for people or information.

Process Cycle Efficiency

Viewing the process cycle efficiency (PCE) for a practice is also helpful. Allowing for an 80 percent analysis (think time) and/or approval wait time, a PCE of 20 percent or greater for I-work can be considered acceptable. PCEs of less than 20 percent should be considered improvement targets. The PCE for Case Study 4 are shown in Figure 6.6 for the procedures associated with Task Management. Speeding up delivery by tuning the efficiency of the work is a primary target of Lean Production.

Delivery Velocity, representing the effectiveness of the delivery, and Process Cycle Efficiency, the speed of the delivery combine to build an image of the information flow within the practice and associated procedures. If the delivery is slow and the cycle time poor the turbulence is most likely high.

Velocity and PCE metrics should be run first at the practice (or function) level and be requested for all procedures within a process if there is an indication of slow or unacceptable delivery speed. Velocity reports represent the central tendency of the deliverables velocity of the total reporting audience. For a procedure, the velocity number references the central tendency for all deliverables within the procedure. For a practice area, this number references

Process Cycle Efficiency score:	16% Overall
*Define—Operational Tasks:	2%
*Define—Administrative Tasks:	5%
Track Tasks:	16%
Issue and Record Tasks:	25%
*Represent Opportunities for Improvement	

FIGURE 6.6 Process Cycle Efficiency Scores for Task Management in Case Study 4

*Represent opportunities for improvement.

the central tendency for all procedure deliverables within a practice area.

Meter Impact: Unacceptable velocity indicators are signals that you need to examine the information workflow variables that can be adjusted to improve the situation.

EXAMINING UNHEALTHY PROCESSES

If the Sigma and delivery indicators are not favorable, the next step is to examine the value stream associated with the practices and procedures, looking for improvement opportunities. At the procedure level, each group should work through a brief valuation workshop. Examining each procedure by outlining the targets and potentials for improvement, as demonstrated in Figure 6.7, is helpful in discovering non–value–added elements of the workflows.

Procedures are prone to being influenced by many variables that can impact overall work performance. The analysis process will allow managers and I–workers to highlight work behaviors, the purpose of the work, and the specific deliverables for each critical procedure they participate in during the course of a normal work cycle. This data is then used during a value stream analysis to determine opportunities for improvement. Diagramming a work procedure is relatively simple once you establish a common map for the data you have collected. Using the mapping structure in Figure 6.7 and the data collected in Case Study 4, we can see how the work behavior translates into the *challenge* column, the work objective or purpose provides the basis for the *cause* column, and, of course, the deliverable fills the *impact* column.

During the analysis session, each target (procedure in the practice or functional area involved in the work scenario under study) is ranked based on the risk posed to the overall

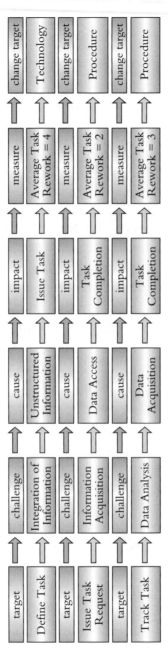

FIGURE 6.7 Value Stream Workshop—Productivity Opportunity Mapping

work scenario delivery. Figure 6.8 presents a simple risk analysis model that can be applied to each procedure (target) within a target work scenario.

Balancing the risk factor and the PCE for each procedure within a work scenario will allow management to determine the procedures most in need of improvement. In the example of task management shown in Figure 6.8, "defining task" had a PCE of 3 percent and a potential risk factor of 7.2 out of a maximum of 5 (based on a 5-point scale for each factor), representing a 28 percent risk factor. Risk ratings for other procedures within the Task Management work scenario were between 5 and 20 percent, with PCEs of 16 to 25 percent. Defining the task became the focal point of the improve analysis for the core team seeking to improve task management at the base.

To manage risk properly, companies need to know what risks they face and the potential impact on their information flow. Often they don't. Each industry has different types of risk; each company thus should develop a taxonomy that builds on these broad risk types. Some organizations would flag any risk associated with production whereas others would flag high-risk numbers associated with sales, for example.

A company must not only understand the types of risks it bears but also the impact of these risks on the business. Less obviously, it should understand how the risks that different business units take might be linked, and how they may impact the overall level of risk for the organization. In other words, companies need an integrated view of operational risk factors. One way of gaining information transparency is through an integrated risk view. Creating a risk table by risk type will help. This table should be broken down by risk category and show the burden each business unit bears along with an overall view of the cumulative risk by category. High concentrations of risk aren't necessarily

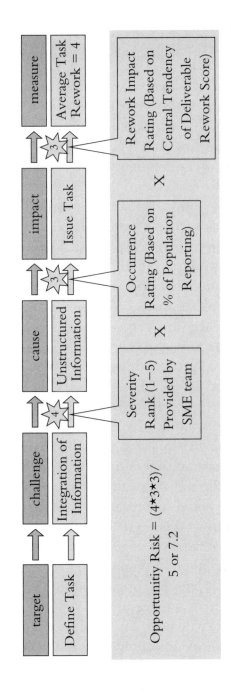

FIGURE 6.8 Risk Analysis for Procedures

140

bad. Everything depends on the company's tolerance for risk. Unfortunately, many companies lack the data to articulate such a risk strategy.

Looking at the enterprise and business unit priority ratings and the risk factors shown in Figure 6.9, you might assume pipeline security would demand top priority. Further review of the situation reveals that the PCE for pipeline security is above average whereas rig maintenance is suffering from low PCE and fairly high risk factors (compared to delivery management). Interviews with the business owners might reveal concerns over aging equipment that are not visible at the enterprise level. The low PCE on rig maintenance, combined with the high risk factor, would outweigh its lower enterprise priority. Determining which work scenarios warrant attention requires balancing multiple objectives against need. The heart of a procedure-based risk analysis is the capability to define action and the resulting ability to direct process improvement. Many organizations build risk analysis plans, but only a few subject matter experts or business or project managers are involved in the process. Often the results of these activities are not embraced by the larger organization. Building on the collective thinking of a statistically significant number of people across the organization vests confidence in the risk analysis and the core team's recommendations. This risk analysis model may

Enterprise Priority	Business Unit Priority	Work Scenario	Risk Factor	Process Cycle Efficiency (%)
3	4	Inventory Maintenance	150	5%
2	2	Pipeline Security	500	28%
4	1	Rig Maintenance	400	7%
1	3	Delivery Management	200	13%

FIGURE 6.9 Risk Analysis Sample

look simple, but it is a very powerful tool when applied well. It helps the team assess stakeholder issues and concerns, identifying and creating improvement plans that move the enterprise as a whole forward.

INTEGRATION OF PRODUCTIVITY AND PERFORMANCE

The third layer of the measurement pyramid is information flow (IF) indexes. The variables within IF consist of work alignment, technology alignment, and quality. Our initial measurement discussion focused on delivery. When the delivery indicators raise red flags, where do you look to resolve the challenges? A good starting point is the assembly-line work elements. Since the I-work assembly line is invisible, we measure the variables that interact to enhance or hinder the flow of information (which makes up the raw materials of our deliverables). We look at the gap between the work behaviors that are expected and those that are performed and the gap caused by utilization of enablers of those behaviors (the technology and procedures to be performed). In each case, we seek to clarify any gap between the expected and the actual performance.

When examining these variables, our goal is not only to identify the gaps but to determine if the expected flow is appropriate for the work being performed. These issues are generally worked out during one or more POM sessions. These sessions focus on clarifying the target procedures, including their overall value to the function, their order of performance, and their priority (with regard to functional deliverables).

Exposing the structure and expected behaviors relating to a given work scenario establishes the foundation for business continuity and work transparency

Productivity Capability Measure

The Productivity Capability Measure (PCM) produces a view of information flow and technology utilization. PCM provides us with a quantitative view of the variables that impact our ability to do I-work: work behaviors, work distribution, technology alignment, and utilization. Flow and utilization views are built based on the procedures assessed. These views may be incomplete if an insufficient population of participants within a work scenario has been assessed.

In the PIF model, all work procedures within a given work scenario are statistically analyzed to create a set of complex indexes that may include:

- Work-technology index
- Technology utilization
- Technology effectiveness by procedure
- Work distribution by role
- Work effectiveness by procedures

Properly utilizing and supporting labor is the most challenging aspect of I-work productivity. Results of the initial I-work productivity impact assessment shown in Figure 6.10 demonstrate the work behaviors for three types of I-workers within the task management work scenario (Case Study 4): managers (information brokers), experts (SMEs), and operations (integrators). The figure presents the estimated current model for all three workers in task management. The average misalignment with the desired state is 43 percent, with the greatest gap generated by content generation and asynchronous communications work behaviors.

An unhealthy work scenario generally demonstrates challenges in work distribution as well as technology support. In the case of the task management work scenario,

	Managers Task Model (%)	Task Estimated Current State (%)	Experts Task Model (%)	Task Estimated Current State (%)	Operation Task Model (%)	Task Estimated Current State (%)
Content	20	40	25	40	35	25
Communication	25	20	20	20	15	35
Collaboration	20	15	20	25	20	10
Search	10	5	10	5	15	20
Problem Solving/Analysis	20	10	25	10	10	10
GAP		45		40		45

FIGURE 6.10 Work Distribution for Task Management, Three-Role Model

Figure 6.11 shows technology misalignments as well. The responses from all three types of workers, demonstrated that they continue to use personal communication tools. The research indicates that the managers should be migrating toward collaboration tools, the expert works toward desktop functions and the operations team toward content generation tools. Though these are broad categories the index shows a strong mis-alignment in the technology being used to accomplish the work.

Determining the technology gap requires a quick look at the mapping of the association between work and technology support most often used by the workforce. Each technology in Figure 6.12 has been associated with its corresponding I-work mode to make it easy for the team to select the most appropriate capabilities. Broker/Coordinators (e.g. managers) should use collaboration support, for example, as their primary technology with Desktop computing as their secondary support tool. To improve work flow for Transactors the team would select Core Technologies

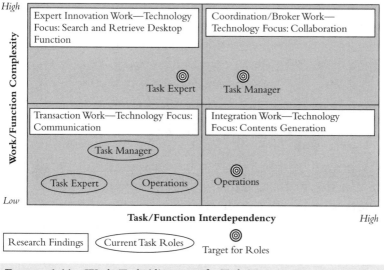

FIGURE 6.11 Work-Tech Alignment for Task Management

(e.g. e-mail or search engines) over any form of collaboration. Once again the right tool for the right job is critical.

The diagram shown in Figure 6.11 is based on research developed over the past four years that provided a technology–work alignment model. The research demonstrates that roles are associated with varying degrees of usage of different technologies, as outlined in Figure 6.12. The communication requirements and information processing needs of the different types of I-work can be vastly different. Business environments with *higher complexity* are characterized by large volumes of information processing, volatile and uncertain business conditions, and a lack of structure in the underlying work. *Highly interdependent work* requires frequent synchronization and coordination of the agents involved in the I-work. While office productivity and basic communication applications may suffice for transaction work, highly interdependent but less complex integration work would benefit from core communication and enterprise application technologies. More complex invention/innovation work, however, involves highly volatile information, unstructured tasks, and a large volume of information processing. We hypothesize that group collaboration technology might be more appropriate there. Finally, coordination work is characterized by both high complexity and high interdependence and may find all three classes of technologies useful.

In summary, as complexity and interdependence rises the greater the benefit from collaborative technologies. The power of collaborative technologies will be diminished if the work requires minimal interaction among the players. The better the fit between the type of technology and the type of I-work, the greater likelihood for improvement in performance experienced by the firm.[1]

Technology	I-Work Roles			
	Expert	Coordinator	Transactor	Integrator
Core Communications Technologies (CCT), which Includes E-Mail, Search Engines	Secondary		Primary	Secondary
Group Collaboration Technologies (GCT) which Includes Groupware and Online Team Spaces, VOIP, and Mobile Computing		Primary		
Enterprise Computing Technologies (ECT), which Includes Enterprise Software Applications such as CRM, Business Intelligence Software, and Document Management Systems			Secondary	Primary
Desktop Computing Technologies (DCT) which Includes Standard Office Software (Word Processing, Spreadsheets, Presentation, and Personal Data Management Tools)	Primary	Secondary		

FIGURE 6.12 Technology—I-Work Role Alignment

Source: Krishnan, Ibi

In Case Study 4, the assessment data demonstrated that the overwhelming use of e-mail as a technology support mechanism continues to enforce procedures that the organization is rapidly outgrowing.

CONCLUSION

While two of the predominant attributes of the knowledge ecosystem are complexity and interdependencies, two of our prime business objectives are to provide clarity and simplicity. Therefore, we continually seek better ways to visually represent the ecosystem and its needs and characteristics. The goal at this stage in the project is to provide a widely accepted vision for the business and the technologists to build upon. Throughout the course of building a PIF, the overarching goal is make the framework intuitive and supportive of a *people-ready business.* A people-ready business, as Steve Ballmer, chief executive officer of Microsoft Corporation, explains, "is one that ensures its people have the tools that empower them to become ultimate drivers of business success. It gives people the support, the resources, the permission and the tools they need to solve business problems decisively."[2]

All participants must be able to easily see how the image is built and how much they influence the results. PIF is about people designing productive information-centric work situations that allow them to be highly productive.

ENDNOTES

1. Vish Krishnan and Indranil Bardhan, "The Impact of Information Technology on Information Work Productivity," September 30, 2004.
2. Steve Ballmer, "Microsoft Announces New 'People Ready Business,'" VisionPRB Launch News Release, March 7, 2006.

◈ 7 ◈

Balancing the Equation

Driving innovation within an enterprise is linked to the ability to empower people. An innovative enterprise is a people-ready business that drives success by improving the ability of the workforce to deliver value to customers. The heart and soul of a people-ready business is it's ability to support the workforce through technology, procedures, and training to meet the productivity and quality requirements of the business strategy. Organizations are looking for more flexible and far-reaching ways to serve their customers and constituents. At the same time, they find themselves hampered by legacy procedures and technology infrastructures that challenge their abilities to transform their operations and to cope with workforce gaps. Organizations must find new ways to think about processes and systems to transform their business ecosystem.

When you think about transformation and operational excellence, you think about innovators such as Southwest Airlines, whose unique service model allowed low-cost air travel to become a reality, or a Wal-Mart, which connects seamlessly with its suppliers and trading partners. Innovative use of technology allowed both companies to rethink the traditional business model and produce winning scenarios. Process innovators, such as British Telcom (BT), that have driven information access to the fingertips of their customer service agents drive market share and competitive advantage through workforce enablement. Unique utilization of technology and streamlining of procedures allows faster quality delivery and improved shareholder value. Like any transformation, these are not quick fixes; rather they must be anchored in comprehensive plans to develop a managed and forward-thinking infrastructure that can support the current and future demands of the business.

Business really is, in some senses, a never-ending cycle of discovering insights, figuring things out, making decisions, sharing goals, collaborating in teams, and taking action. As shown in Figure 7.1, business is balancing the needs of the enterprise with the demands of the customer to satisfy the stakeholders. Innovative customer-centric enterprises focus on the value-generating processes and alignment of tools that facilitate their work. In world-class, people-ready businesses,

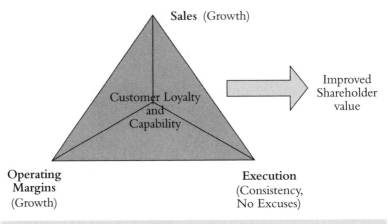

FIGURE 7.1   Performance Balance

it's not just about the standard processes for doing work, it is about gaining that extra insight, providing information workers (I-workers) with the ability to make that exceptional decision, and handling the exceptions in the operational process well, not just routinely. It is important to keep this balance in mind when establishing objectives and goals for any productivity improvement project.

ESTABLISHING THE LONG-TERM GOALS

Traditionally enterprises that find they have a performance gap (often expressed as a productivity or profitability gap) will seek to close it by either scaling back the market's expectations for future earnings—an approach that implies an acceptance of lower stock prices (and might get them fired), or improving baseline earnings to meet or exceed the market's expectations.

Shareholders and managers alike prefer the latter course, so the question is how to get there. Companies can find additional earnings in two ways: They can try to improve operating performance by squeezing more profit out of existing capabilities, or they can improve corporate performance by organizing in new ways to develop initiatives that could generate new earnings. By pursuing both of these approaches simultaneously, companies can take a powerful organizational step toward meeting the challenges of today's hypercompetitive global economy.

It is not enough simply to demand increased returns from existing capabilities. Reducing the workforce or asking for more production without changing the approach will yield diminishing returns and eventually become counterproductive.

Productivity Impact Framework (PIF) focuses on developing an open, secure, and manageable process and technology infrastructure that supports operations today and over time. Improvement solutions need to address the requirements of the demands presented at the operational level for a work scenario as well as the interoperability at the enterprise level. Improvement plans should work together with tools, technologies, standards, and benchmarks that help make the solution work within the ecosystem.

Leadership must inspire performance improvement and control the risk associated with change. Management must provide guidance, through programs such as PIF, to build continuity with a company's overall strategy and values. Too often, attention is focused solely on formal systems and processes, such as organizational structures, budgets, approval processes, performance metrics, and incentives. Exceptional performance improvement can be realized with a mix of procedural and technology improvements. Balancing the need for operational efficiency with the desire for effective delivery should be the goal of every leadership team. Prioritizing and communicating the high level-objectives (listed in the "Drivers" column of Figure 7.2) of operational efficiency, procedure improvement, or high-performance culture (innovation and quality) is the outcome of a leadership analysis of organizational goals. Determining the right set of goals requires the leadership team to first work on the current year strategies (e.g. improving time to market for new products or faster decision making as shown in Figure 7.2) required to meet the financial and operational objectives of the organization. Setting strategies allows the larger management team to review, at a high level, the organizational capability to meet the strategic goals. Combining this deliberate prioritization, from the top down, with a solid communication plan and improvement program will foster understanding and dedication to efficiency/effectiveness (E/E) balance within the workforce.

Drivers	Strategies	Efficiency/Effectiveness Capabilities
Operational Efficiency (Delivery Speed)	Business–Shared Services, such as Finance, Accounting, Legal, etc.	• Data Integration Rather than Duplication • Integration Process Workflows • Shared and Integrated Calendar and Scheduling
	Process Optimization and Integration	• Flexblity and Ease of Use of Information and Transactions across Applications and Repositories • Common, Consistent Tools and Practices
	Financial Management	• Analyze and Report Relevant Data • Activity/Role–Based Dashboards
Procedure Improvement (Value Stream)	Time to Market New Products and Marketing Programs	• Availablility of Information Where Needed, When Needed • Automation and Notification, Reducing Manual Interventions • Remote and Off-line Access to Information and Transactions
High-Performance Innovative Culture (Productivity)	Collaboration	• Activity/Role–Based Dashboards • Workflow; Collaborative Review
	Faster and Effective Decision Making	• Real-Time Access to Analysis and Reports • Approval Process: Notification and Subscription

FIGURE 7.2 Balancing and Supporting Efficiency/Effectiveness

Business leaders should set a realistic pace for change. Companies with otherwise successful plans often stumble by moving too slowly on strategy or too quickly on organizational change. Sequencing and pacing are often difficult to judge; the factors that affect them include management's aspirations, external market conditions, and the organization's capacity to execute a number of productivity improvement initiatives simultaneously. Decisions about the pace of change influence how many initiatives a company runs as well as their complexity. In a short-term turnaround situation, it is hard to run more than 4 or 5 key initiatives; in many cases, 2 or 3 are preferable. However, in a two- to three-year corporate-performance improvement program, 15 to 20 corporate-wide initiatives may be necessary. Aligning initiatives with the larger corporate goals is critical to overall success of the program. If the current emphasis is on operational efficiency a team can be assembled to examine multiple work scenarios seeking efficiency opportunities that will operate on a common platform. Effectiveness, procedure improvement and high-performance culture, initiatives tend to more unique and, thus, are generally run one work scenario at a time.

IMPACT OF PRODUCTIVITY IMPROVEMENTS ON FINANCIAL PERFORMANCE

Understanding the impact of performance-level improvements on the enterprise requires taking a look at how the performance measures are also related to the time-honored financial metrics. Outlined in Figure 7.3 the conclusions from recent studies indicate that stakeholders should take a closer look at return on asset (ROA) and return on equity (ROE) while continuing to look at the traditional efficiency improvement targets (profitability, profit, and sales growth). As Figure 7.3 demonstrates, effectiveness improvements driven by investments in technologies such as collaboration services (e.g. instant messaging and web-based conferencing) and procedural improvements (e.g. strategic outsourcing and work balancing with vendors) that impact work quality are most likely to improve ROA indicators before they appear in the profitability or growth numbers.

Good corporate governance dictates that investment relationships are validated during the design phase of PIF

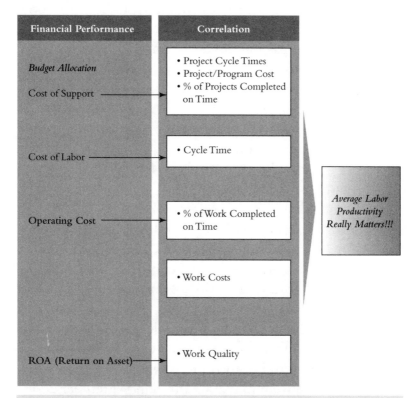

FIGURE 7.3   Performance Measures to Financial Metrics

Source: Vish Krishnan, and Indranil Bardhan, "The Impact of Information Technology on Information Work," Information Work Productivity Council (IWPC) Annual Research Report, September 27, 2004.

project and certainly before the measurement phase is begun. Investments, for technology or organizational improvements, require that business managers can point the board of directors and other stakeholders to the standard metrics that they intend to improve. The correlation of assessment results to financial metrics gives stakeholders an appropriate bellwether by which to judge the success or failure of investment and improvement programs.

Since the correlation of assessment results to the financial metrics is taken from relatively new research, I have included a summary of two research programs that provide a solid evidence of this correlation. These studies, like other research in business management, make no attempt to provide an all-encompassing model of company performance. The target of both studies is to expose the impact of information work and its supporting technology on firm-level financial performance.

The first project was undertaken by the Information Work Productivity Council (IWPC) from 2002 through 2004. As executive director of the IWPC, it was my privilege to guide this research council of technology industry vendors (including among others Microsoft, Cisco, HP, SAP, Intel, Accenture, and Xerox) and the academic community (including among others the University of Texas—Austin and Dallas, MIT—Sloan School of Management, Harvard, New York University—Stern School, and the University of California—Berkeley), working with the business community, in developing a deeper understanding of work in the information-centric economy. The IWPC study was led by Professor Vish Krishnan of the University of Texas—Austin from mid 2003 through September 2004. This portion of the study focused primarily on the correlation of the I-Work performance measure to firm-level financial metrics.

The study by Frost & Sullivan Research (sponsored by Verizon and Microsoft) is an interesting correlation of one information-work (I-work) behavior—collaboration—to company market performance. These and other similar studies have established a growing awareness of the impact of I-work on financial performance. The bottom line is to carefully consider the impact you wish to have on your organization before launching an assessment project. If you have been charged with reducing operating cost, you will look toward improvement projects that reduce overall cycle time and/or reduce the cost of labor (downsizing or down-skilling, reducing the required skills needed through cuts in the workforce or automation). These projects would keep stakeholder attention firmly focused on the standard profitability metrics. However, if your target is to improve customer satisfaction, employee retention, innovation, or product quality, you will want to emphasize projects that improve effectiveness. Improving effectiveness certainly does not eliminate efficiency gains, but such projects should have stakeholder attention focused on ROA, ROE, and earnings per share (EPS) metrics.

REVIEWING THE RESEARCH

The IWPC Study[1]

The study by Vish Krishnan examined I-work assessments against a project management work scenario for 1,200 participants (representing a bottom-up view of performance measures). The research team then analyzed objective financial measures from 180 companies (predominately based in the United States) associated with the participants.

The productivity assessment polled the respondents on the impact of technology on their projects and firms over the last four years. The study compared these findings to the financial metrics to understand the relationship among technology, associated I-work behaviors, and deviations from established trends in financial data.

The analysis examined the relationship between the performance measures (e.g., information technology usage, subjected ratings of effectiveness and efficiency, as well as a limited number of structural and process variables) collected through the assessment and the aligned financial metrics. Krishnan summarizes the results in this way:

- A reduction in cycle time is significantly correlated with improvements in a firm's gross margins.
- Improvements in quality and on-time delivery rate are correlated with improvements in a firm's operating margins.
- Improvements in quality, new product sales, and on-time delivery rate are correlated with improvements in a firm's return on assets.
- An increase in new product sales is negatively correlated with change in a firm's return on equity.
- A reduction in costs is correlated with an increase in a firm's earnings per share.

This study offers considerable support for and credibility to the performance measures used in the qualitative assessments (which are similar in context to those used today in the PIF studies). The study provided statistical evidence of the relationship between the I-work behaviors and technologies represented in the PIF assessments to the long-term financial metrics of an enterprise.

Krishnan clearly pointed out that I-work behaviors and technology impact different financial metrics. Effectively aligned I-work behaviors had a significant positive impact on performance measures. Highly efficient use of technology had a significant positive impact only on cycle time, cost, and completion measures. Krishnan summarized his findings in this way:

- Effectiveness has a significant impact on improvements in a firm's gross margin, operating margin, and ROA. The impact of effectiveness on a firm's EPS is weaker, although it is significant.
- Efficiency has a significant impact on improvements in a firm's ROE.
- The propensity of firms to use technology has a significant impact on improvements in ROA and ROE. That is, firms that are leading edge users of technology realize significant improvements in ROA and ROE compared to firms that are late adopters.
- Autonomy in making I-work–related decisions and setting goals is significantly associated with improvements in firm EPS.

Reviewing the balance between the impact of I-work behaviors (the way we work) and the supporting technology showed that technology alone does not produce significant productivity gains. The study reviewed results from all companies studied, regardless of their tendency to use technology (the self-professed leading edge users as well as the laggards). The results show that the impact of information technology (over the procedure improvements) on financial performance is not statistically significant. Again, this finding confirmed the earlier conclusions (but through objective financial data) that I-worker–related technology alone does not have a direct impact on performance by itself, but its impact is strongly mediated through I-work behaviors. As a result of this study, the research team established that productivity of I-work can be measured and validated using the efficiency and effectiveness constructs discussed earlier.

The Frost & Sullivan Study

The second study of interest was a unique study of 946 decision makers (presidents, vice presidents, directors, and managers) representing small, medium, and large enterprises in the United States, Europe, and the Asia-Pacific (representing a top-down view of performance).[2] The study audience included participants in five major economic sectors: healthcare/pharmaceutical, government, financial services, manufacturing, professional services, and high tech. The key finding of this study was that collaboration is a key driver of business performance. The statistical analysis of the data, shown in Figure 7.4, indicated that collaboration is twice as significant as a company's aggressiveness in pursuing new market opportunities (defined as strategic orientation). Additionally, it is five times as significant as the external market environment (defined as market turbulence).

The primary goal of this study was to examine collaboration across geographic regions and key industries. The significance for our discussion is not just that business leaders view collaboration as a key business driver, but that these beliefs were validated by a correlation to financial results. Frost & Sullivan found that the corporate culture and structure along with the technology support accounted for 59 percent of the variance in company performance.

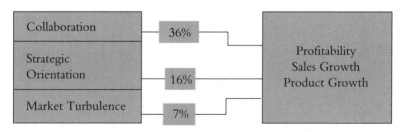

FIGURE 7.4   Global Collaboration Model

Source: Frost & Sullivan, "The Global Collaboration Index", April, 2006

As with the IWPC study, Frost & Sullivan compared the perceived performance values set by the participants to their competitors (much worse to much better). This proven approach correlates well with actual performance.[3] The comparative analysis, as opposed to adjusting raw financial measures of performance, allows more easily for us to view industry and regions differences. "The significant impact of collaboration on labor productivity, customer satisfaction and on product development, innovation, and quality implies that a holistic program that directs and measures the benefits of collaboration, and related investments and resources, to reap these performance benefits should be adopted by companies."[4]

Figure 7.5 graphically demonstrates how collaboration influences the financial metrics of profitability, profit growth, and sales growth. In this study, collaboration was a strong driver in the process-level performance measures (which influence the financial metrics), including labor productivity, product development, customer satisfaction innovation, and product quality. Though this study focused on only one I-work behavior, collaboration, as with the IWPC study, this study underscores the relationship of I-work behavior on the financial performance of the enterprise.

INVESTING IN GOVERNMENT

As the U.S. Air Force case studies discussed earlier demonstrates, the effectiveness and efficiency gains realized by streamlining the think factory is not limited to for-profit enterprises. The Organization for Economic Cooperation and Development (OECD) has described recent innovations in procedure, training, and technology as major driving factors in administrative reform programs in nearly all governments in OECD countries. New ways of thinking about the business of government have led to

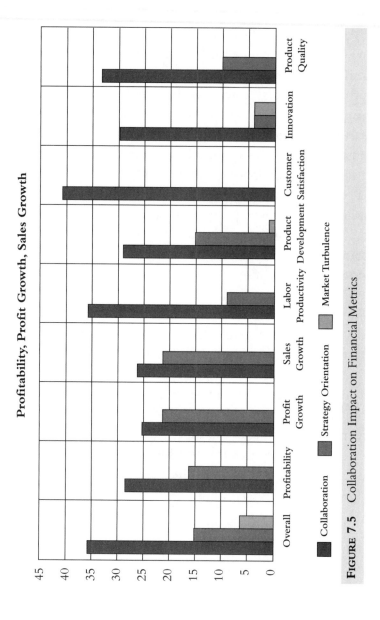

FIGURE 7.5 Collaboration Impact on Financial Metrics

groundbreaking changes in policy and the way governments operate.

The concepts of e-government, or technology- (specifically web-) enabled government, have come to the forefront in most public sector agencies. Recognizing that the business of government is delivering public services, e-government is really about implementing a spectrum of technology-enabled strategies to:

- Achieve agile and responsive policy advice and service delivery
- Strengthen transparency, collaboration, and financial accountability of government agencies to constituents
- Enhance the ability of agencies to function effectively in the global arena
- Achieve transformation and efficiencies in administration and oversight

Effective e-government improves customer service by streamlining processes and making communication and staff collaboration more efficient. The Frost & Sullivan study indicated that governments were not leaders in the adoption of collaboration techniques. When adapting new solutions to the operational challenges of governing, e-government initiatives must balance the risks to security and citizen privacy. I-work communication and collaboration improvement solutions for the public sector are rapidly addressing these concerns and enabling public agencies to embrace more innovation solutions.

The world of government is becoming more complex with increasing demands on the processes and technology infrastructure to support existing and emerging business interactions. The public sector needs improvements in efficiency as well as effectiveness. The solutions must develop employee knowledge and skills in concert with the technology improvements. Innovation comes from ideas, and the human infrastructure of government supplies the ideas. However, in both developed and developing economies, the forecast is that governments will face a workforce skills shortage. Various estimates predict that between 23 and 50 percent of the government workforce in developed economies will retire over the next ten years.

Before that time, government agencies will need to ensure that their procedures and technology support are working in concert to provide a solid knowledge transfer and efficient operation for a newer and smaller workforce. For some agencies this will require a great deal of change and innovation.

While changes in government operations will lead to new processes and tools, they will also lead to policy and procedures changes that will impact citizens. Solutions implemented by government agencies must reduce operational complexity as well as simplifying information exchange with citizens.

SHORT-TERM MEASURES: FOCUS DOWN ON WORK SCENARIO BENEFITS

Establishing the link between strategic (long-term) metrics and performance measures is the next goal. Attention, motivation, and participation in productivity improvement projects can be generated by building a strong and direct connection between enterprise strategic directions and operating objectives. The goal here is to provide a better working understanding of performance measures and the challenges you may encounter building them. Many work scenarios have outcomes that are extremely difficult to measure because their outputs (deliverables) are hard to define. The U.S. Office of Management and Budget (OMB) describes these complex deliverables as:

- Many incremental deliverables that are nested inside of (or contribute to) larger outcomes
- Results that will not be achieved for many years
- Administrative or process oriented (rather than specific deliverables)[5]

Addressing these and other issues relating to building reasonable and realistic short-term performance measures is the next step in the process of defining objectives. I have included some of the examples provided by the OMB as they provide a variety of simple-to-understand case studies in performance measures that are useful to those in the public sector and relatively easy for those in the commercial sector to translate.

The closer the work is to the production line, the easier it is to define the deliverable. For example, if the goal is a customer-ready contract, the performance measure could be simply to count the days from order to delivery. If this is the only measure in the scenario, all eyes, and measurement, will focus on the word processor and the contracts administrator printing off the completed document. Unfortunately, this measure will not account for the research work subscenario that had to be completed prior to the administrator constructing the contract or the customer service agent estimating the costs. Although a tangible asset was completed by the final procedure (constructing and printing the contract), there are hidden, or uncounted, I-work subscenarios that must be accounted for if we are to have full measure of performance. If the overall delivery velocity or process cycle efficiency (PCE) was determined to be low, the team would be seeking to improve the number of contracts going out the door. If the financial metric was to increase profitability by increasing productivity, the team might be looking to reduce the labor cost of production. In both cases, we would need to account for all the deliverables (tangible and intangible) and work within the production line—including all the work and deliverables in the subscenarios.

As you think about building performance measures, consider the importance of both the tangible and the intangible deliverables required to complete the final deliverable. Productivity improvement is focused on improving customer satisfaction with the delivery. All work scenarios have customers, internal or external, that determine if the final delivery velocity and the quality are satisfactory. In the automobile factory if you expect to assemble a finished car you must make sure all the sub-assemblies are built and delivered before you start the assembly line—the same is true in the think factory. A customer-ready contract can not be produced if the you have eliminated the subscenario for gathering and validating required pricing quote. Value streams and performance measures are dependent on identifying the interim as well the final the customer and the deliverable.

Work Scenario Outcomes Difficult to Measure

Consider the situation where the work scenario outcomes are extremely difficult to measure. The outcomes of some programs are inherently difficult to define (the value stream) and measure. Programs designed to address strategic planning or foreign policy objectives might fall into this category. By focusing on why a program is important and what makes it difficult to measure, sometimes we can define the scope of the problem more specifically. Going through this process may also identify the root of the difficult-to-measure work scenario. Such scenarios also tend to include a large number of customer-related procedures (e.g. often check points or customer validation meetings); in Six Sigma terms, these may be the root cause of productivity loss.

Performance measure challenges can often be traced back to fundamental questions about the program. When reexamined, these questions may yield insights into better ways to assess effectiveness. As mentioned earlier, one way to reexamine those issues is to relentlessly ask *why*:

- *Why* it is important that staff is dedicated to this work? What would we lose if the work was not done? How would you know?
- *Why* are program operations important?
- *Why* does the program do what it does? If the program were fabulously successful, what problem would it solve?

This line of questioning should help clarify the work scenario's true purpose and its desired outcome, which should help you determine what really needs to be measured—in essence, the actual value-producing deliverable. For example, the purpose of a work scenario may be to support a global partnership. In trying to define a performance measure, it might be helpful to ask "*Why* is the success of that partnership important, and what role does the work scenario play in achieving that goal?"

It also can be helpful to identify what core issues make measurement difficult. For example:

- The work scenario's purpose is not clear.
- The beneficiary or customer is not defined. Who are the direct and indirect beneficiaries? Who are the long- and short-term beneficiaries? If overhead (or the government in public sector) does not do this, who would pay for it?

- Stakeholders have a different view of the work from work managers. How would stakeholders be affected if the work was not done? Are there performance measures for stakeholders that shed light on the work's effectiveness?

Some programs are difficult to measure because data is not available. To help address this situation, ask these questions:

- Why is data unavailable?
- What data is available?
- Can we fund the cost to find data?
- If data is not available, are there proxy measures that will indirectly measure the program's outcomes?
- Do stakeholders have data that they generate to track the program?

If quantitative data is unavailable (no current workers are doing the work) or inappropriate (there are no current processes or established procedures for the work), consider using qualitative data, such as completing only the top-down Productivity Opportunity Map (POM). For example, in assessing the quality and speed of issuing orders in a military unit (as no uniform method is used across all operating units), a POM may be useful, and could complement output measures such as speed of delivery (from request to delivery).

Work Scenario as Part of Larger Program

Consider the challenge of the work scenario that is one of many contributors to a larger program. Often several work scenarios (or programs) from a corporate level (or federal government), business units (various levels of government: federal, state, local), or partners (private sector or nonprofit) all contribute to achieving the same goal. The contribution of any one work scenario (or program) may be relatively small or large. Examples of situations with these characteristics may include enterprise-wide strategic planning, international peacekeeping, just-in-time assembly planning, or highways upgrade programs.

One approach to this situation is to develop broad yet measurable outcome goals for the collection of deliverables while also having program-level performance goals. For a collection of work scenarios guided or directed at central or summary level (a board of directors or a federal agency, perhaps), a broad outcome measure may be one of the goals in a group or agency strategic plan (e.g., increasing the home ownership rate). The broad outcome goal often can be tracked using enterprise or national data that is already being collected, while the program-specific goals may require more targeted data collection. Both the broad outcome goal and the work scenario–specific goals could be addressed in an aggregated PIF report, but only the work scenario level measures would be addressed by the assessment.

Research and public service investments are generally considered difficult to measure. If solid performance support criteria were applied to such programs the assessment team can establish an agreed upon outcome measure.

 OMB EXAMPLE 1

Several federal education programs, totaling nearly $14 billion, contribute to helping children learn to read. One of those programs, Reading First State Grants, provides about $1 billion to help implement proven literacy reforms in schools with low reading scores.

Program outcome goal: Increase percentage of children in high-poverty schools reading proficiently by the end of third grade.

Work scenario goal: Increase percentage of at-risk third graders receiving Reading First services who can read at or above grade level.

It is important to *right-size* the measure to match the work level. Sometimes a work scenario (or program) has a significant contributor, or leverages so many dollars, that an appropriate goal is an enterprise-wide or societal outcome. Programs in education or corporate research often fall in such broad reaching categories. Other times it is more appropriate to write measures specific to unit or group beneficiaries. There is no rule of thumb on where that threshold is. I can only suggest that similar work effort, or a similar percentage contribution to the desired outcome, use similar measures. This will allow the enterprise to aggregate measures at a few summary points, such as business units or regions.

Often broad reaching outcomes can be focused on one or two long term output statistics. Answering the *why* questions listed earlier will help the team identify the key performance indicators (KPIs) that provide solid evidence the program is moving toward a successful outcome for the organization. In a commercial enterprise product development is given milestones by which to measure program success. Product incubation is given a window of time before it must produce a marketable output—not hard to measure if the KPIs for the product are clearly outlined for the team. Incubation projects are often funded from Research and Development (R&D) business units, while products receive approval and funding from production business units.

In the fast-paced world of computer gaming a research team maybe given a few weeks to complete a story line and demonstrate an action packed prototype to the marketing team for audience testing and production for mock up. Depending on the target market the researchers will have a set of KPIs to meet that might include the level of violence level and genre. If the specific KPIs are met, the concept will move to a production development team and the next set of outputs including layout, game location, character definition and graphics definition. These interim outputs serve to assure the business leaders that the ultimate outcome—a marketable video game—will be met. The R&D group may have five game concepts under review to every one project in production. The departments must coordinate their objectives and long term goals to keep the company profitable. The same staged approach can be used when addressing the output and outcome definitions for research and social service programs as shown in OMB Example 2.

 OMB EXAMPLE 2

Several federal programs provide student aid so that low- and moderate-income students can afford to attend college. Of these, only the Pell Grant program and the loan programs contribute a large enough share of student aid to merit a societal outcome. The Pell Grant program provides grants to nearly one-third of all college students, while about half of all students receive loans from or backed by the federal government. In contrast, the College Work Study program reaches only about 6 percent of college students, and so the OMB recommended that the measures relate to the program participants only (as shown in the long-term measures):

Federal Pell Grant long-term measure: College enrollment gap between low-income and high-income high school graduates

College Work Study long-term measure: Rate of College Work Study students who complete their postsecondary education program

Sometimes work scenarios are best designed, as demonstrated by the OMB college grant example, to work together toward a common goal, but each provides a different piece of the service or activity. In other cases, work scenarios, as in the case of the video game development, are designed to merge funds and support the same activities as well as goals; this is particularly true when various business units or agencies all contribute resources (funding, people, or technology) to reaching a common goal.

When programs fund different activities and do not co-mingle funds, work should be able to develop activity-specific performance goals that support the broader outcome (e.g. profitable sales or service delivery). It is likely, however, that these will be output goals. The challenge will be agreeing on how each of the separate activities contributes to the outcome.

When programs do co-mingle funds in support of a goal (imagine if the same business unit did the video game concept work and the production work), it is extremely difficult to assess the marginal impact of a dollar since all funding supports similar activities. Programs may seek to claim responsibility for the entire outcome and output, despite having a shared, and sometimes small, role in the overall activity. However, you should seek to evaluate whether such claims are realistic. It may be useful in such situations to consider measures such as unit costs in terms of output per dollar spent as well as the output per combined dollars spent.

The goal of collecting performance information is to answer three basic questions:

1. Is the overall effort working?
2. Are there outcome measures for the overall effort/ program?
3. Are there evaluations?

Is the enterprise-level contribution making a difference? Because withholding funding as an experiment is not a viable option, consider whether there are other ways to see what would happen in the absence of top-down funding. Can you compare current funding to an earlier time when there was no corporate or federal funding? Are there business units, or regions of the country, where there is no corporate or federal funding?

How is funding effort shared between various levels of the enterprise and/or partners? How does the distribution of funding effort compare to measures of need or the distribution of benefits?

Scenario Where Results Will Not Be Realized for Years

In some cases, the outcome of a work scenario may not be realized for many years. Often this problem can be addressed by identifying meaningful output-oriented milestones that lead to achieving the long-term outcome goal. Many research and development (R&D) programs, such as a new operating system, hydrogen technology, and Mars exploration, fall into this category.

To address this issue, a program, as described in OMB Example 3, should define the specific short- and medium-term steps or milestones to accomplish the long-term outcome goal. These steps are likely to be output-oriented, preliminary accomplishments on the path toward the outcome goal. You can construct a roadmap to identify these interim goals, then suggest how they will be measured and establish an evaluation schedule to assess their impact on the long-term goal. It is important that these steps are meaningful to the program, measurable, and linked to the outcome goal. In other words, long-term goals are not sufficient for measuring current activity.

OMB EXAMPLE 3

The purpose of NASA's Mars Exploration program is to explore Mars, focusing on the search for evidence of life. To that end, NASA, as the overall business owner, defines spacecraft missions, which provide one level of measures (an outcome) to assess program effectiveness: mission success. Further, within each mission (such as the Mars mission), the program develops technologies; builds, launches, and operates robotic spacecraft; and performs research using the spacecraft instruments. While these steps take many years to complete, they provide many milestones against which a mission—and the program—can be monitored. Useful output measures could include timeliness in achieving certain steps as well as percentage cost overruns.

It may also be useful to track process-oriented measures, such as the extent to which participants make decisions based on competitive review. For example, research programs can have many uncertainties, including their expected outcomes. Therefore, while research programs are encouraged to define measures that can track progress, not all will be able to do so. Such programs may rely, in part, on process measures, such as the extent to which the program uses merit-based competitive review in making awards.

To qualitatively address the research itself, some programs develop measures to reflect meaningful external validation of the quality and value of the program's research. To address the uncertainty of research outcomes, programs may also be able to demonstrate performance in terms of the broad portfolio of efforts within the program. Expert independent evaluators might also help determine if the process of choosing appropriate long-term investments is fair and open and promises higher expected payoffs in exchange for higher levels of risk. Rotating evaluators periodically may help ensure independence and objectivity.

Another solution is estimation of future results using computer models or expert panels. The Environmental Protection Agency, for example, uses computer models to estimate cancer cases avoided.

Administrative Work Scenario

Finally consider the work scenario or program that is administrative in nature. Many programs in business and government are administrative or process oriented. Administrative work scenarios tend to present a number of problems when it comes to measuring performance. One issue is the appropriate balance between outputs and outcomes. Realistically, output measures may be useful for evaluating the efficiency of internal process-oriented activities. In cases such as the investment in computer infrastructure, for example, the spending may be better evaluated with other capital asset evaluation tools (e.g., a return on investment or total cost of ownership) than a performance improvement assessment. However, for larger administrative efforts, consideration should still be given to ultimate outcomes and delivery. In some cases, it may make most sense to evaluate the administrative costs as part of the overall program rather than as a separate activity. For example, a government grant program (such as the Pell Grant program in OMB Example 2) may contain separate accounts for the grants themselves and for administrative salaries and expenses, yet both accounts might be viewed as providing inputs into a single program. Similarly in the commercial space, many business units, such as sales, marketing, or product development (such as the video game group), could use the data stored in a new corporate data warehouse. Subprograms could be evaluated that provide

unique data views for each of these business units and ultimately reflect back on the core data warehouse.

As many administrative functions run across business
units or agencies, the development of common measures
should be encouraged. A good example is the U.S. Air
Force (Case Study 1) Human Resources team. Unique
measures could be built for this team, though they served
the entire Air Force, they had definable outputs that could
be used to measure the teams productivity. Building performance measures that drive operational excellence while
meeting strategic objectives is often a difficult balancing
act. This single act, at the outset of the project, is critical to
the overall program success.

CONCLUSION

Improving I-work productivity has been a major challenge
due to the intangibility of I-work outcomes. As a first step
in gaining a deeper understanding of its role and business
value, we focused first on the strategic goals: Why do we
need to improve? Is the goal efficiency—reducing cost and
overhead—or effectiveness—improving customer satisfaction through quality work and innovation? These goals can
be complementary if they are related to how work is being
accomplished and what technology is being utilized in the
course of doing the work.

Just as in an industrial factory, balancing the complexity
and the interdependence of I-work with the supporting
technology is the key to building highly productive teams.
Technology can drive some efficiency gains, but the impact
of technologies on process-level work production is strongly
impacted by the effectiveness of the information work
behaviors (the way we work) within the individual work
scenarios.

Current research demonstrates that effectiveness is an integral and statistically valid measure of the productivity of I-work, and it explains a significant portion of the variance in a firm level financial metrics. Effectiveness of I-work has a significant impact on improvements in firm level operating and gross margins as well as on ROA and EPS. Efficiency of I-work has a significant impact on a single measure of firm performance: ROE. In general, we can say that information technology needs to be implemented with the intent of maximizing work and financial outcomes, in a manner that fundamentally improves the work behaviors of the firm, which, in turn, will improve the performance measures and financial metrics. Neither public nor private organizations will realize significant performance improvements if they use technology only to improve quantity of outputs and inputs, ignoring the quality of the outcomes. Effectiveness should be as much of a focus as efficiency. Unfortunately, currently efficiency tends to drive productivity improvement decisions. Successful productivity improvement projects focus the alignment and definition of performance measures on work scenario deliverables that will ultimately meet or exceed customer expectations.

ENDNOTES

1. Excerpts and charts quoted from Vish Krishnan and Indranil Bardhan, "The Impact of Information Technology on Information Work Productivity," September 30, 2004.

2. Frost & Sullivan, "The Global Collaboration Index: Measuring Sustainable and Competitive Collaboration and Its Impact on the Performance of Companies," April 11, 2006.

3. Conant, Jeffrey, Michael Mokwa and Rajan Varadarjan. "Strategic Types, Distinctive Marketing Competencies and Organizational Performance: A Multiple Measures-Based Study," Strategic Management Journal, (Sept, 1990), Vol. 11, pp. 365-383.

4. Frost and Sullivan, Ibid., page 21.

5. OMB Program Assessment Rating Tool (PART): Office of Management and Budget, 2004.

Part Three

BRIDGING
THE GAP

The key to competitiveness is responsiveness. Today organizations are placing the highest priority on technology-related efficiency and effectiveness (i.e., using technology to help the workforce harness creativity, collaboration, and control though communications and constantly improving productivity). Technology-driven efficiency is only one aspect that contributes to continued competitiveness. The challenge of the information-centric economy is to have the ability to manage in a state of continual change, constantly adjusting resources to meet rapidly changing business demands. The ecosystem is no longer contained within the legal walls of the enterprise; survival in the modern marketplace requires the ability to leverage all forms of resources across the entire supply chain, the ability to extract more value (for the same or less asset investment) from the virtual workplace. A major driving factor for business and government leaders today is addressing this three-pronged challenge—productivity (more output per unit of input), innovative capacity (the best mix and balance of resources), and value chain leverage (combining assets)—easily, quickly and flexibly.

To understand why some organizations derive greater financial value from using the same business structures and information technologies than others, my colleagues and I have analyzed numerous organizations and identified a few key practices for more effective decision making. Among these practices, we have identified three common characteristics of top-performing companies:

1. A shared vision of the valuable opportunities that exist across the enterprise and within individual business units or agencies
2. Good business planning for nearly all initiatives
3. Effective and open communication across the organization regarding the strategy and operational plans

The Productivity Impact Framework (PIF), along with traditional financial tools such as return on investment and net present value, facilitates the definition of value for an initiative as well as its alignment with the organization's critical success factors. The ultimate goal of this process is to enable the organization to make optimal use of its resources within the context of acceptable risks.

A key catalyst for the effective application of these practices is the efficient creation of a business benefits statement and an economic justification or value proposition for the business investment required to carry out the improvement. An easily implemented best practice is to view the value proposition not simply as a static document but as a dynamic mission-critical tool used for the improvement of business governance within the organization. As Robert McDowell, Vice President Microsoft Corporation, states in his book *In Search of Business Value*, "Technology provides no benefits of its own; it is the application of technology to business opportunities that produces ROI."[1]

Where do we go from here? We have talked about the challenge, how to identify its root cause and how to assess it. The remaining question is how to respond. Shaping the improvement plan and looking forward is never simple unless you have a map. Identifying the business objective and measuring the productivity gap, as shown in Figure PIII.1 should be considered the first stage in the process. Building a prescription for success is the critical next step.

To this point, we have talked only about the diagnosis: discovering the baseline and defining the current state. In the next three chapters, we spend some time discussing prescription in chapters 7 and 8: translating the measures into improvement maps and preparing to measure success. As we look forward, business continuity and data transparency have become important issues in corporate governance and public trust today. In Chapter 9, we discuss how PIF, as a business framework, can help organizations achieve these goals.

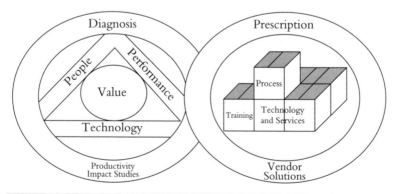

PIII.1 Linking Diagnosis and Prescription

ENDNOTE

1. McDowell, Robert, and Simon, William, In Search of Business Value, Select Books, Inc., 2004.

8

Imagining the Future

The world has changed dramatically in recent years, and companies are confronted with an environment they have not seen before. New strategies, structures, and operating practices are required to manage change and create and sustain advantage. Businesses need to make faster, more informed decisions—communicating and collaborating immediately and effectively no matter where employees are located. They need to better understand and serve their customers globally. They need to interact seamlessly with suppliers and distributors. They need to seize market opportunities faster than their competitors. They need to be more efficient than ever. In short, companies need business agility to succeed.

FINDING THE SOLUTION

There's no doubt that efforts to make information work more productive are increasingly on the radar screen. But we've been trying to crack the productivity code for a long time. From 1997 to 2003, U.S. companies spent two-and-a-half trillion dollars on [technology] largely in an effort to make themselves more productive. Still, white-collar productivity hasn't improved all that much in the past decade. For example, if you look at the financial and services sectors of the economy where almost 20 percent of the technology spending has taken place, there has been no decline in the overall cost of managing the business since 1996. At GE, Jeff Immelt says despite all that was spent on IT, over 40 percent of the company is still in administration, finance, and backroom functions.

On a macroscale, technology has made work almost unmanageably complicated. The average workday in the United States has expanded to about ten hours, but workers are at peak productivity only about half the time. Between 60 and 80 percent of people say they often can't find information they need to make good decisions. In fact, I have developed a 90-90-90 rule that says 90 percent of the information I get I toss, 90 percent of what I save I never read again, and 90 percent of what I want to find again I can't find.

In our view at Xerox, the problem is this: IT dollars have been spent automating the world of data, which is a particular kind of information structured for processing by machines. It has largely not been spent on the world of the document, where information is presented for human understanding and action. Therefore people have largely been left out of the IT equation, except perhaps when it comes to the potential for reducing headcount.

Source: Jim Firestone, Vice President, Xerox Corporation, presentation at the IWPC Forum, February 2, 2003

CLOSING THE GAP

What is the key to driving business agility? Leading companies agree that a key component of the answer is technology. They view technology as a strategic asset that must be integrated with their business strategies tuned to support their unique processes: integrating the business and technology architectures. Technology is artfully integrated into the business model to enhance employee productivity, to streamline inefficiencies, to launch new products and services, and to squeeze even more efficiencies out of the supply chain. The best players in any sector of the economy understand this integration and invest in procedure and technology improvements when they can, increasing customer satisfaction, market share, revenue, and long-term profitability. These companies, however, also say that technology needs to be more manageable, flexible, and cost-effective.

The perspective taken here is that technology should enhance, not encumber, the business—and that the right application of technology should make this happen. There must be a business and a technology architecture, and these views must be integrated so that they enable companies to design and manage a unified infrastructure as a core part of their business.

Closing productivity gaps requires streamlining from an employee's desktop to the back-end servers that run the business with:

- *Flexible connections across the business.* Software that connects your company's information, people, systems, and devices quickly and cost-effectively so your workforce has the agility to act as one unified business
- *Streamlined business procedures.* Methods that, when combined with the technology solution, multiply the power and impact of your people so your business has, by being more flexible and efficient, greater capacity to "do more faster with less resources"
- *A dependable business infrastructure.* Technology that enables you to build a flexible highly reliable business infrastructure that's high quality, reliable, and secure, that removes the barriers to information flow across the enterprise

- *Best economic business return.* Establishing a total business ecosystem that enables you to reduce cost required to maintain day-to-day operations and free up investment for new capabilities to drive profitability

Our next goal is to develop a means to bridge the gap between the diagnosis, as described in Part II, and the improvement plan or prescription. Here we review an approach to building consensus around the business and technology architectures that underpin an improvement roadmap.

BUSINESS ARCHITECTURE

Information-centric business processes and the technologies, that facilitate and integrate them within the enterprise, are growing in numbers and complexity. To make the right choices, you need to establish five related factors. The Productivity Impact Framework (PIF) process drives the first four:

1. Define the information value stream (as outlined in Chapter 5).
2. Establish the work complexity and interdependency requirements for the work scenario (as shown in the Work-Tech index in Chapter 5).
3. Establish a common language or taxonomy for mapping the work scenarios within a process/practice are together (an output of the assessment process described in Chapters 6 and 7).
4. Define the information dependencies within each procedure and between work scenarios in the value chain (part of the deliverables taxonomy established in the assessment).

The fifth factor is defined during the improvement process and should include your technology department, training department, and potential vendor if new technology is added to the environment:

5. Establish business architecture and corresponding technology architecture for the improvement project and the relationship to the larger enterprise architecture.

This last step will allow your technology department to integrate your needs into the larger enterprise picture. In this way, the solution will serve your current business needs and work well with other technology used in your organization.

Technology (software solutions and hardware) does not integrate itself. It takes vision and clarity to integrate multiple business needs into a unified ecosystem that can support the diverse and collaborative needs required in the evolving information-centric workplace. Business leaders have often been frustrated in their efforts to communicate with technology departments and vendors the needs of the business. Technology providers have recognized this need as they see their own businesses and products growing in complexity and connectivity potential. In response, Microsoft and other leading edge vendors are transitioning toward a business services orientation. Microsoft is asking its own Microsoft Consulting Services and partners to be "more like business consultants than computer science experts ... more concerned [in the initial phases of the discussion using methods such as PIF] with what the customer wants to do than how to engineer it."[1]

Driving delivery speed and quality is the highest priority of the business leader. Ensuring the right balance between efficiency and effectiveness that improves creativity, collaboration, and control is the desired state. Figure 8.1

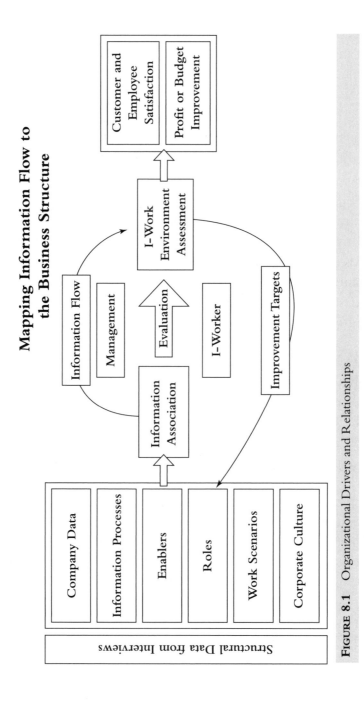

Mapping Information Flow to the Business Structure

FIGURE 8.1 Organizational Drivers and Relationships

reviews some of the major relationships and challenges improvement projects must balance to be successful. Enterprise ecosystems are dynamic in nature; therefore, they require a process of continuous improvement and revitalization to support growth and innovative change. The relentless drive to discover the greatest need (or pain point) within the system encourages both agility and the ability to continually adjust resources (people and technology) to respond to changes in business and market drivers while leveraging the organizational value chain to react efficiently and effectively.

Building a business unit architecture and mapping the underlying technologies allows for the development and delivery of solutions based on business need while remaining in concert with the larger organizations ability to provide support. However, there are many challenges to this simple statement: Complex technology environments where business workflows often transcend many layers of the technology architecture, different types of software and hardware, inconsistent standards and proprietary solutions from extended interorganizational workflows that must now cross architectural boundaries all add complexity. The information need, defined by the baseline assessment for an individual business unit, may even require communication, collaboration, and data transparency outside the enterprise firewall with vendors, suppliers, and customers.

Each work scenario is a network of behaviors, people, and organizational processes collaborating across internal and external space. To establish and communicate needs, there must be a unified and enterprise-wide standard approach for developing and presenting the business requirements. This common framework, as outlined earlier, will facilitate the mapping of business needs to core technology capabilities for accurate, fast, and flexible implementation of the process models within an enterprise. The key to this mapping is a common language (taxonomy) used to describe and categorize the needs.

Chapter 2 outlined the need to discover the intersection of the business process and the work that is performed. To drive the process business architecture, you need to take a step up in your view—that is, you must make sure that you have a clear navigational map of the enterprise, business unit, and functional area that accounts for internal and external information links.

A clear understanding of relationships between work scenarios, at an enterprise level, provides guidance on the impact of proposed changes. The enterprise diagram in Figure 8.2 clearly shows that a requested change to the customer relationship management (CRM) system would potentially affect at least four major process areas—order processing, sales, services, and customer support—and those impacted processes have the potential to affect numerous work scenarios. This is not to say that change is impossible because it is complicated. Rather it points out that it is important to understand the organizational, financial, and productivity impact your requested change might have on the larger ecosystem.

The model shown in Figure 8.3 starts to integrate the enterprise technology and business structures with the work behavior model established by the productivity assessments. The taxonomy concepts outlined in Chapter 3 are used in such environments to bring together what might otherwise be disconnected concepts.

Using a common language helps everyone associated with the business to understand its goals and challenges. Standardizing on a common set of architectural diagrams and a common language used to reference the business components that appear on the diagrams will help everyone understand and respond to your proposals. In Figure 8.3, the relationship between the technology infrastructure,

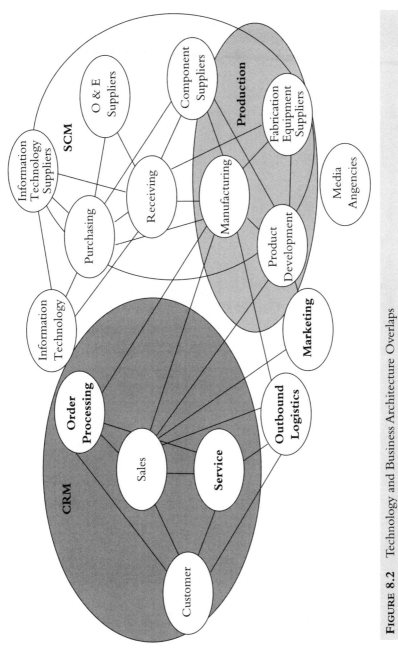

Figure 8.2 Technology and Business Architecture Overlaps

Source: © 2003—4 META Group, Inc., Stamford, CT

191

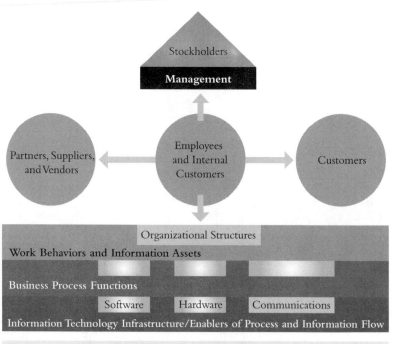

FIGURE 8.3   Common Language Establishes Integrated Architecture

represented by the vertical cylindars in the background, the business functions, and the associated work behaviors depicted by the horizontal connecting bands, is clear. The diagram shows the value of the impact that the combined structure delivers to a wide variety of internal and external participants and stakeholders. Building an architecture for an improvement plan within a large ecosystem is a complex but necessary endeavor to achieve the productivity gains the business requires.

WORK SCENARIO BUSINESS ARCHITECTURE

An integrated enterprise business and technology architecture can be used to focus the improvement planning at the work scenario level. The core taxonomy used to express the business needs should be centered on work behaviors required to deliver on the business unit mission. The taxonomy is used to describe the intersection of process and practice (where organizational structure and processes come together) with the performance of work. Earlier we discussed that the taxonomy of information work is comprised of five behaviors:

- Content generation and management
- Communication (asynchronous)
- Collaboration (synchronous)
- Research (search/retrieve)
- Problem solving/analysis

Work production, in an information-centric work scenario, is dependent on the consistent, clear, and uninterrupted flow of appropriate information. To reduce the turbulence of that flow, we need to identify bottlenecks and improve the work behaviors at the process-practice intersection. The next challenge to a productivity improvement project is to identify the business architecture required for the target work scenario, as shown in Figure 8.4.

Once the business requirements, in terms of actions needed (e.g., archiving or aggregation), are established for each required work behavior, the team will be ready to review options for improvement. Some requirements can easily be filled by existing technologies or by restructuring procedures. Introduction of new technology and/or streamlined procedures should be carefully aligned to communications and training programs for the impacted information workers.

In the Korean Air case study, we were able not only to identify needed technology improvements but to associate those improvements with procedural changes and workforce training. As noted in Figure 8.5, the team recommended restructuring some key procedures and providing

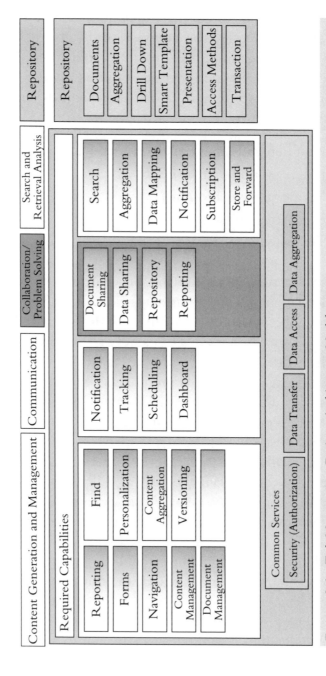

FIGURE 8.4 Task Management Business Architecture Model

Source: Courtesy Microsoft Corporation. Based on design by Dinesh Kumar, Microsoft Consulting Services.

194

Taxonomy	Challenge	Recommendation	Training	Technology
Technology and Information Flow	↻ Limited use of communication collaboration, and search/retrieve features impacting I-work.	☑ **Improve the effectiveness of I-worker information flow.** ☐ **Training** in advanced features targeting collaboration, search/retrieve, is recommended to improve the outputability of I-work in Finance, Sales, and Maintenance. Additional training in collaboration and search/retrieve features reccomended for all functions. ☐ **Training** in document management techniques and software features. ☑ Expand use of template-driven documentation.	☐ Train managers to encourage and support **utilization of targeted technologies.** ☐ Train all functions in the use of **document management and version control.**	☑ Add, or make available, e-mail, scheduling, and workflow software with **collaboration, search/retrieve and communications features.** ☑ Shift to **fully integrated desktop technology suite.** ☑ Utilize **document versioning and collaboration technology** (e.g., that offered in Sharepoint Portal). ☑ Create **intelligent templates** or smart documents (such as those created with Info Path).

FIGURE 8.5 Improvement Recommendations for Korean Air

training to the entire workforce. The decision by Korean Air to change the supporting technology was a bold step designed to deepen its investment in the quality of labor.

Determining the procedures and features to improve is a matter of reviewing the results of the baseline data and the business requirements established at the beginning of the project. A useful tool for evaluating the improvement targets is the process cycle efficiency (PCE) calculation developed from the assessment data. Simply put, the PCE represents the average percentage of time effectively used by the work team for a given procedure. PCE scores of less than 10 percent should be targeted for immediate improvement work; scores between 10 and 20 percent should be targeted for longer-term improvement. The sample PCE scores in Figure 8.6 are based on the analysis

Task Management	Velocity	PCE (%)
☑ Define— Administrative Tasks	0.05 Tasks Defined/Hr	5
☑ Define— Operational Tasks	0.01 Tasks Defined/Hr	2
Issue Tasks	1.25 Tasks Issued/Hr	25
Track Tasks	0.06 Tasks Tracked/Hr	16
Record Tasks	1.25 Tasks Recorded/Hr	25

FIGURE 8.6   Air Force Task Management Process Cycle Efficiency Sample

of a task management work scenario in Case Study 4, the Air Force Base Task Management project. The core team reviewing the results elected to focus their improvement project on the 'Define Administrative and Define Operational Tasks' (denoted by the checkmark symbol in the chart) of the work scenario as a means of improving the overall PCE score of 14.56 percent.

Working backward from the PCE score, the team noted that the low velocity (production of deliverables) in the "Define" procedures for both administrative and operational tasks was too slow. The baseline assessment data linked the slow delivery in both procedures to a 60+ percent rework challenge. As part of the value stream analysis described in Chapter 6, non–value-added procedures are identified and analyzed. Reducing the rework in these procedural areas is a primary target of the process improvement. This team has targeted its technology improvement at data transparency. Procedural change can be effected at the lower levels of the organization, but changing the way management provides information will take some time. To promote improved throughput, the team has elected to build a collaboration site and reward the use of this site and its associated tools. Since the target was the shaping and defining of a task (or order), the team focused on content management and aggregation as well as the search function from the list shown in Figure 8.4.

Engaging both the business owners and the technologists allows the core team to translate the specific requirements of the business from the value stream analysis onto the architecture diagram. The needs, such as notification or content aggregation, are aligned to the business behavior driving the need (regardless of role). Once the core diagram is completed, the technology department is then invited to add additional requirements for its side of the business, such as repository or security services.

The business architecture mapping exercise allows all the interested parties to come together to discuss the challenges using the common taxonomy that drives the improvement roadmap. At this point in the process, the technologists are called upon to assist the core team in associating the business architecture, similar to the diagram in Figure 8.4, with a high-level technology architecture. The technology architecture diagram in Figure 8.7 is the one associated with the improvement project at Korean Air. The improvement project team was able to demonstrate the relationship between the requirements for improvement in content generation and management as well as collaboration with the recommendation by the technology department to change the messaging and portal technology.

Some improvements, as discussed previously, will be procedural; others will involve new or unique uses of existing technologies. Most improvement roadmaps require a combination of both procedural change and technology support. Regardless of the improvement, it is important to build a clear and direct connection between the streamlining needed in the business and the technology improvement project. All changes must lead back to the value statement made in the value stream analysis at the conclusion of the baseline assessment.

CONCLUSION

The measures and improvement roadmap provide a well-rounded image of the productivity capability and needs within the target work scenario(s). When all work scenarios within a target process or practice area have reported results, the measures provide a complete composite view of the process/practice area. In the U.S. Air Force case study (Case Study 4), the majority of the work scenarios (two out of the three information request functions) had been

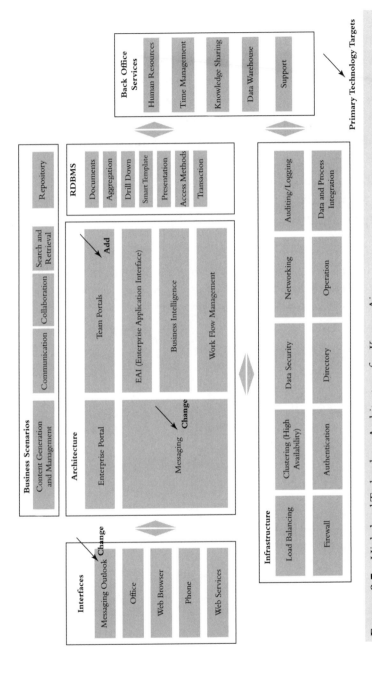

FIGURE 8.7 High-level Technology Architecture for Korean Air

Source: Courtesy Microsoft Corporation. Based on design by Dinesh Kumar, Microsoft Consulting Services.

199

assessed prior to the start of improvement mapping. Thus, the combined metrics were considered representative of the factors that contribute to improved customer satisfaction and process efficiency. Using the explicit and subjective data results as guidelines, the core project team and business leaders select an improvement roadmap that will target the key challenges within the offending procedures. Recognizing the challenges of the poorly performing procedures allows the organization to target process and technology improvements to produce a positive impact: removing the barriers and improving the overall information flow.

ENDNOTES

1. Michael Hickens, "Microsoft's Role for Business Solutions," March 31, 2006, *www.internetsolutions.com*, and *www.microsoft.com/businesssolutions/ navision/demos/integrated_innovation/index.html*.

❧9❧

Performing in Public

The concept of the Information Economy has been talked about so much lately that it is no longer a startling fact; in many quarters it is simply a given. Most managers are concerned about not only how to manage the power of information, but how to leverage it as a competitive advantage. Although information is one of the most renewable resources an organization has, it is also an organization's most elusive resource. The technological advances in global connectivity, managing information density, and the increasing speed of transmission represents more of an organizational challenge than anyone would have imaged. The lifeline of the Information Economy is tied to the use, creation, management, and transmission of information. Gauging organizational health and vitality requires a more consistent, repeatable, and scalable measure of the flow, quality, and support of organizational information. The Productivity Impact Framework (PIF) provides us with many of these signposts. At the enterprise level, it is important to reconsider *why* and how the Information Economy issues impact profitability, financial management, and stakeholders.

BUILDING PROFIT IMAGE

Perhaps the most interesting attribute of information work (I-work) is its capability to leverage the ability of organizations to mobilize and exploit their intangible assets: people, processes, technology, and the knowledge generated by them. Intangible asset leverage has become far more important and decisive in the Information Economy than investing and managing physical (tangible) assets.[1] In an extremely competitive global economy, companies see increasing pressure to cut costs and to increase productivity and innovation. John W. Kendrick, George Washington University economist, in his studies demonstrated that business investment trends at the close of the twentieth century had reversed themselves, with intangible rather than tangible assets consuming the majority of the investment dollars.[2] Kendrick noted that brick-and-mortar tangible asset investments are now growing by only around 31 percent whereas business investments in intangible assets are growing by nearly 63 percent. Managing this new strategy requires that organizations measure the business value of the investment. An organization's ability to leverage its content and exchange information to increase employees' abilities to deliver and establish relationships will be a major difference between those that thrive and those that lag or go out of business. Most organizations are acknowledging these economic facts and recognizing that they have much to learn about how best to manage and optimize their investment in organizational capital. Organizations talk about investing in their people capabilities; they establish overhead budget line items relating to knowledge management, training, and procedure improvement; but they receive little, if any, systematic feedback on the economic value of their investment and even less information about how to improve the value produced by their investment. For I-work to become a recognized contributor to business value, methods for identifying, categorizing, and measuring the behaviors that promote accountability and increase productivity must be established within every enterprise.

Current accounting practices view activities related to human capital as an expense without direct relationship to revenue production.[3] This is a challenge because it results in financial statements that do not supply all the information investors need to measure a company's value and can call into question the benefit received from a budget investment in I-work productivity. The accounting systems behind the financial statements we see today continue to focus solely on a company's tangible assets. As a result, current financial statements, and the metrics that feed them, fall far short of providing the needed information about the large investments in I-work support time and funding for procedure improvement, knowledge and management development, and innovation. The most interesting aspect of broadening the definition of intangible assets from the semitangibles—patents and trademarks—to include business methods (the way you do business) or the innovative use of tools (technology) and even the most elusive—goodwill, is the opportunity to broaden the value statement. The value proposition for the measurement, monitoring, and improvement of people-centric intangible assets is made clear when we compare the results of a company that relies on patents for its market potential (e.g. Lucent Technologies) and one that includes unique business processes for its market edge (e.g. Cisco).

CISCO SUCCESS STORY

Using Core versus Context [examining the flow of information versus the content of the information] approach, we have streamlined the company. We had to deal with out-tasking issues that were [within the company] core but the function was not core. This required real focus but the results show the benefits:

Applying these principles—using Internet solutions—we produced benefits of $2.1 billion for Cisco in FY 2003. That includes savings of:

❖ Customer care 920 million

❖ Workforce optimization 800 million

❖ Supply chain management 270 million

❖ E-learning 140 million

Metrics are essential: The key question was how to measure I-W [information work].

1. We must measure both quantity and quality in our productivity calculations.

2. The consumer or target of the production defines the outcome value, i.e., "impact."

3. To make optimal decisions, we should look at sets of inputs and outcomes, not individual variables. The productivity of a business letter is not very interesting, until one puts it in the context of the costs and impact of different kinds of business communications.

Gary Bridge, Cisco Corporation, CIO, speaking at the IWPC Forum, February 2, 2004

Lucent Technologies notes in its company literature that it has over 18,000 patents. This treasure trove of patents could not provide the market edge to keep Lucent a leader in its field as Cisco and other competitors increased their customer base by developing innovative new business processes. Cisco has increased its intangible asset productivity in excess of the conservative 10 percent per year ($2.1 billion in 2003 alone) in the past few years through innovative new business processes, including opening its knowledge base directly to registered customers. Cisco empowers customers to solve their own problems, reducing customer care calls and improving response time. While Lucent looked to its large legacy of patents, Cisco enticed investors with lower cost and increased market share. A strong sales force and a unique management vision has become a stronger market driver than a jungle of patents or the weight of physical buildings.

We discussed Wal-Mart earlier in the field of retail innovation. Intel Corporation's manufacturing capabilities demonstrate a similar astonishing result. Its "Copy Exactly" method of ramping up new factories is quick and efficient, and allows Intel to duplicate yields from existing plants and decrease time to market. "In 1997, VLSI Research estimated that revenues per manufacturing employee increased from $114,000 in 1985 to $461,000 in 1995. Meanwhile, the company's revenue increased by three times during those 10 years, while the number of factory workers decreased by 30 percent."[4] This approach to manufacturing is not patented. The unique application of engineering and management capabilities, intensive information sharing, and the ability to replicate procedures is one of core ingredients in Intel's secret sauce.

Merely staying in business has never created star performers. It is the consistent innovative leadership in the core competencies, including management, not patents, buildings, or even capital, that creates outstanding performance. All tangible and semitangible assets can be copied (or worked around) or replicated. The key for outstanding performance in the coming years will be the strength of the information-centric workforce. The failure to sustain and retain successful information workers (I-workers) can constrain a company's growth opportunities.

The bottom line is that when you're trying to determine how to make a company thrive relative to its rivals, you need to look beyond physical assets and identify, measure, improve, and report on its core performance.

STAYING IN BUSINESS

Leading and managing is not about just turning a profit. Managers often forget that making that profit is intrinsically tied to maintaining the trust and confidence of employees and customers. Improving productivity is often limited by external rules and regulations. The U.S. Federal Drug Administration requires pharmaceutical companies to document not only the outcomes of their drug tests but all outputs including conversations, analysis, and support materials. As mentioned earlier, introducing instant messaging as a productivity tool to reduce e-mail traffic and speed up collaboration is an outstanding idea but not viable without conversation tracking and a records storage mechanism in place. Managing the dual challenges of regulation versus productivity will continue to challenge business and government leaders.

Corporate Governance

Corporate governance is an international concept that can be translated as management and control. The phrase is a collective term covering a company's behavior and customary practices in several areas, such as management practice, mechanisms for management and control, board of director ethics, and shareholder policies. Company rules representing a minimum of what the company's various partners may expect governs several of these areas. Seen in conjunction with the demands from international and national partners for continuously profitable commercial activities, a company's own goals imply that management will exercise corporate governance beyond the minimum requirements.

RISK IS A FACT OF BUSINESS LIFE

Taking and managing risk is part of what companies must do to create profits and shareholder value. But the corporate meltdowns of recent years suggest that many companies neither manage risk well nor fully understand the risks they are taking. Moreover, our research indicates that the problem goes well beyond a few high-profile scandals. McKinsey analyzed the performance of about 200 leading financial-services companies from 1997 to 2002 and found some 150 cases of significant financial distress at 90 of them. In other words, every second company was struck at least once, and some more frequently, by a severe risk event. Such events are thus a reality that management must deal with rather than an unlikely "tail event."

Directors confirm this view. A 2002 survey by McKinsey and the newsletter *Directorship* showed that 36 percent of participating directors felt they didn't fully understand the major risks their businesses faced. An additional 24 percent said their board processes for overseeing risk management were ineffective, and 19 percent said their boards had no processes. Managing risk requires documenting, analyzing and fully understanding the value stream that is required to manage each process. Since it has been so difficult to visualize and manage I-work it is not surprising so many organizations have a gap in their risk management approach.

Source: Kevin S. Buehler and Gunnar Pritsch, "Running with Risk: It's Good to Take Risks—If You Manage Them Well," *The McKinsey Quarterly*, No. 4 (2003).

Productivity and Goverance

Most executives share the broad view that corporate governance is not a new concept but that the concept is in an evolutionary stage and has not yet found its final meaning. For this reason, our description of corporate governance is also an evolutionary one. Productivity studies are not essentially about corporate governance but are impacted by that governance. Productivity improvement relates to the interface with the company's present and future operations, which is often limited by governance policies.

The recent focus on several areas encompassed by the term "corporate governance" will, in time, show the need for new roles and related responsibilities in the performance of commercial activity. The definition and measurement of organizational capital, specifically the people-driven aspects, is a key component of nearly all these discussions. Metrics on these aspects of the business, based on Kendrick's evaluation, will enhance the ability of investors in all companies to form independent and accurate views as of information-centric enterprises and their true earnings potential.

Governance provides the foundation for the system by which companies are directed and controlled. It deals largely with the relationship among the governing entities of a company—the directors, the board (and its subcommittees), and the shareholders—and their ability to provide insightful and informed governance. Building a dynamic, clear operating image for this constituency allows them to provide the required oversight to the enterprise without being intrusive. Productivity studies can not only provide indicators of productivity of I-work but reveal the way in which the company operates, the current level of operations, and management's vision for improvement. Transparency and accountability are the most important elements of good corporate governance, including:

- The timely provisioning, by companies, of good-quality information
- A clear and credible company decision-making process

PIF studies provide a deeper understanding the information flow, its impact on deliverables as well as the corporate procedures surrounding the use and distribution of information.

An International Issue

In the United States, Sarbanes-Oxley legislation has enlightened many of us on the challenges of managing a business concern. Other areas of the world have expressed concern as they watch the U.S. business community deal with the outcomes of the Enron scandal and other lapses in corporate governance. Establishing methods and means to measure and monitor even the rudimentary elements of information flow required for good governance is difficult, especially when dealing with large enterprises and complex work. In Europe, BASEL II observers have commented that defining and quantifying operational risk metrics that are tailored to individual lines of businesses will be one of the major challenges faced by financial firms in the coming years. Most companies are already examining and documenting the processes they will use to meet the requirements of Sarbanes-Oxley regulations. Financial regulators in the United States are adopting only some of the Basel II accords—but the adopted areas are very complicated. Institutions with $250 billion in assets or more than $10 billion of total foreign exposure on their balance sheet are required to comply by 2007. Enterprises will need to create the proper incentives so that management and other stakeholders not only develop transparent initial approaches but also ensure that those approaches incorporate the concept of continuous process improvement.

GLOBAL IMPACT

Hewlett Packard (HP) operates in 178 countries with approximately 142,000 employees. As Thomas Friedman asks in *The World Is Flat*: "It is the largest consumer technology company in the world; it is the largest IT company in Europe, the largest IT company in Russia, the largest IT company in the Middle East, and the largest IT company in South Africa. Is HP an American company if a majority of its employees and customers are outside of America, even though it is headquartered in Palo Alto, California?"

Source: Thomas Friedman, *The World Is Flat,* Farrar, Straus and Giroux, New York, (2006).

The corporate governance framework in the United Kingdom operates at a number of levels to guide and manage corporate governance, in a manner similar to Sarbanes-Oxley legislation in the United States. The first level is through legislation, particularly the Companies Act of 1985. This act is being replaced by the Company Law Reform Bill, which is currently being considered by Parliament. The second level is through the regulation surrounding publicly listed companies, enforced by the Financial Services Authority.

U.K. companies are also regulated through the Combined Code, which is overseen by the Financial

Reporting Council. The Financial Reporting Council contains general principles relating to the corporate governance of listed companies. Like the Sarbanes-Oxley rules, it requires companies, in their annual report and accounts, to:

- Report on how they apply the principles
- Confirm that they comply with the code's provisions or, where they do not, provide an explanation: hence, the "comply or explain" principle that, if applied effectively, underpins informed dialogue between directors and shareholders

As the world changes, trade and political barriers are lowered, and technology shrinks the connectivity gap, corporate governance becomes a more complex issue. The technology revolution has made it possible to do business anywhere, anytime, with nearly anyone on the planet. As we saw with the Intel example earlier, well-documented business functions can be replicated anywhere in the world. Governance is no longer a local, national, or regional issue. Operating on a global basis requires unprecedented clarity and consistency of processes, practices, and procedures. Developing clear documentation and clarification of the core functions is the first step to consistent operations. Organizations that do not establish a framework for continuous process evaluation and streamlining will most likely treat Sarbanes-Oxley and Basel II requirements as one-time events or as reactive actions to audit. If organizations embrace a philosophy of continuous performance process improvement—examining and aligning people, processes, and technology across the enterprise—meeting Sarbanes-Oxley and Basel II requirements becomes part of an overall improvement and risk management process.

KNOW-HOW ALLOWS REPLICATION

The "Copy Exactly" strategy creates great flexibility for Intel's factory network. Because each factory is nearly identical, wafers can be partially completed in one factory and finished in another, yet yield at the same level as if the wafer were built in only one factory. No other semiconductor manufacturer can do this now.

By creating a global virtual factory network, Intel limits impact from natural or man-made disasters. If an event occurs in one part of the world, Intel manufacturing does not come to a halt. The rest of the factory network is able to continue production and continue shipping product to customers.

Source: Intel Backgrounder, "Copy Exactly" Factory Strategy

Business Continuity

External disruptions to business services from terrorism, natural disasters, and other unexpected interruptions have heightened interest in business continuity readiness from business leaders, external stakeholders, and regulators. The greatest challenge in business continuity is defining I-work–related procedures that may be impacted by a disruption or retirement. The world has become focused on terrorism and natural disasters, but many organizations are facing the imminent retirement of key I-workers. We noted earlier that in the developed economies, such as the United States, estimates are that 23 percent to 50 percent of the current workforce will seek retirement within the next decade. Organizational leadership must ensure that effective controls and procedures are in place to meet these challenges. Creating a value stream analysis for key business work scenarios is one way to start imaging the impact of revolutionary or evolutionary disruptions on organizational capability. Responsiveness to uncertainty is the new benchmark for superior business continuity while also improving I-worker productivity.

Keeping the Information Flow Moving

Superior business continuity depends on procedural knowledge and its use in enterprise practices. Yet I-workers are struggling to cope with increasing rates of complexity while needing to deliver more in a shorter time frame. Organizations want the capability to instantly switch work to other I-workers or locations in a disaster situation without significant loss of productivity. This workforce switchability is dependent on the agility and adaptability of I-workers and their support infrastructure. Using smart forms (semi- or fully automated electronic forms that provide instructions and even fetch the required information on command) is one way to help to drive an informed (I-workers with the basic capabilities are informed of required actions by the software) action-based I-work environment. Modeling, measuring, and proactively supporting the evolution of I-work toward informed action can mitigate some of the looming business continuity issues facing the think factory. Using automation and reducing the need for I-workers to learn the procedural rules that are specific to policy, service, product, and regulation can keep the information flowing and work moving forward.

We would be remiss if we did not mention that mitigating the risk of business disruption requires more than automated forms. Information-centric production must learn the lessons manufacturing learned over the past hundred years: Continuity requires redundancy and backup. We noted that the ability of Intel's organizational capital drives its manufacturing enterprise. The ability to knowledgeably replicate not only production facilities but the associated practices and procedures provides Intel with just-in-time redundancy in the face of disruption. The company balances the ball well, and it is rewarded by the market for it. Automation is not enough; planning, security, and backup are critical.

THE EVOLVING THINK FACTORY

Business must support innovation while managing non-core activities performed by others. Measurement is essential to the dynamic environment if you are to maintain control as you benefit from a truly global environment. Using the concepts found in the PIF as a foundation, you can start the discovery journey by looking at your enterprise ecosystem. Build an image of the information flow and seek ways to reduce the variance in the flow. More important, however, is to create enabling ecosystems in which your virtual work environment understands the value of the knowledge/information cycle, including the central role played by the I-worker, the supporting role of technology, and the reality of the global information-centric economy.

So we have come to the threshold of a radical departure from existing control mechanisms and value systems. The primary driver of innovation is need. Challenges to the way business operates are not new. Mayer Amschel Rothschild, an influential leader in eighteenth-century Germany, recognized the need to change the state of an asset in transit from physical to intangible. In essence, he created the concept of a checking account. As the leader of a large family enterprise, Rothschild had a serious business challenge to solve: Couriers transporting money—gold or silver coin, jewels, or other tangible assets—between family members located across the country were being robbed and murdered. This, of course, meant that the assets never arrived. Solving this problem required a new way of thinking about the nature of money. Rothschild invented checks, which had no intrinsic value but were treated as money; in doing so, he created an information flow. The checks carried the information from one family member to another regarding the amount and person to be given funds from the family banks throughout Europe. The Rothschilds became star performers not because they invented a new theory of economics but because they built the capacity to deliver regardless of environmental disruptions. Now it is our turn to be inventive about the flow of information. To have a positive impact, you must ensure that your innovation is aligned not to the way your enterprise is structured today but to its vision of the future and to the needs of the customer.

The challenge ahead is to create enabling ecosystems. Like the Rothschilds, we need to innovate by putting aside the prejudice of current organizational structures and artificial barriers to information flow. We need to seek an understanding of the ways people work and the way that they should perform work.

It is not about minutes saved but innovation and the freedom to create.

Conventional models of applying technology to information problems have done nearly all they can to improve productivity. To get to the next level, we need to provide people with a better way to work that revolves around the flow of our most valuable assets: information.

All organizations are living systems. A sustained improvement in operating capabilities requires attention to multidimensional dynamics. Technology-only efforts to optimize intangible asset value are not enough; enabling the information flow and making the ecosystem people-ready are the drivers of success. The keys to performance excellence and value creation rest in promoting and enabling the appropriate I-work behaviors and relationships operating naturally within the subecosystems of the organization.

All organizations have inherited challenges and overhead from their industrial era roots. Although we extol the virtues of empowerment, independence, and thought leadership, our organizational behaviors remain locked into the command and control structure of the nineteenth century. Evolution is preferable to revolution, but helping some organizations bridge the generational gap will require more than incremental improvements. Managing transformation is, in reality, our greatest challenge.

As Henry David Thoreau said, "We must walk consciously only part way toward our goal, and then leap in the dark to our success."

ENDNOTES

1. Itami, H. (1987). Managing invisible assets. Cambridge, MA: Harvard University Press.

2. Cited in Laing, J.R., (2000) "The New Math: Why an accounting guru wants to shake up some basic tenets of his profession," *Barron's,* November 20.

3. Lev, Baruch, "Intangible Assets: Values, Measures and Risk," Oxford Press, London, 2003.

4. *Intel Backgrounder,* " 'Copy Exactly' Factory Strategy," www.intel.com/pressroom/archive/backgrnd/copy_exactly.htm.

Glossary

Assets, intangible. Assets that are not physical in nature. The most common types of intangible assets are trade secrets (e.g., customer lists and know-how), copyrights, patents, trademarks, and goodwill.

Assets, tangible. Physical resources controlled by the enterprise as a result of past events and from which future economic benefits are expected to flow to the enterprise.

Baseline. Current state of information work productivity prior to improvement. Baselines set the mark against which improvement is measured.

Basel II. Also called the New Accord (correct full name is the *International Convergence of Capital Measurement and Capital Standards—A Revised Framework*). This second Basel Accord represents recommendations by bank supervisors and central bankers from the 13 countries making up the Basel Committee on Banking Supervision to revise the international standards for measuring the adequacy of a bank's capital. It was created to promote greater consistency in the way banks and banking regulators approach risk management across national borders.

Benchmark. The management process by which organizations evaluate various aspects of their processes in relation to the best practice, usually within their own sector.

Commodity. An undifferentiated product whose value rises from the owner's right to sell rather than the right to use.

Core team. The required team members for a productivity study.

Data transparency. The ability to see all the results or much of the data to ensure there is no distortion of fact.

Delivery velocity. The speed at which products and/or services are delivered to the customer. The unit of measure (minutes, hours, days, weeks, etc.) is generally governed by the deliverable.

DMAIC. Discover, measure, analyze, improve, and control.

Document. Something that contains information. It often refers to an actual product of writing and is usually intended to communicate or store collections of data. Documents might include any discrete representation of meaning, but usually the term refers to something like a physical book, printed pages, or a virtual document in electronic or digital format.

Emerging economy. Term commonly used to describe business and market activity in industrializing or emerging regions of the world.

217

Enablement. To streamline and make work more accessible. Technology-enabled work scenarios deliver results faster and more conveniently, potentially in real time. The transformation typically reduces operating costs.

Hidden work. Work required to complete a procedure that is often done without the end user or consumer realizing the work's contribution to the deliverable or end product.

Information. A message received and understood. In terms of data, it can be defined as a collection of facts from which conclusions may be drawn. There are many other aspects of information since it is the knowledge acquired through study or experience or instruction. But overall, information is the result of processing, manipulating, and organizing data in a way that adds to the knowledge of the person receiving it.

Information aggregation. The ability to combine content from any number of sources into a common venue or distribution channel.

Information-centric work. Work focused on the use, manipulation, transformation, transmission, and/or creation of information.

Information economy. A loosely defined term that characterizes an economy in which informational activities and the information industry play an increased role. The information economy is considered a stage or phase of an economy, coming after stages of hunting, agriculture, and manufacturing.

Information flow. Any tracking of information from source to destination. Information flow affects work structures such as procedures, schedules, or product development.

Information work (I-work) behavior. Includes the five common activities associated with information work: collaboration, content generation and management, personal communications, search and retrieve, and problem solving and analysis.

Information worker (I-worker) types. Include the four basic categories of information work:

1. *Expert work.* Work requiring a high degree of individual knowledge and expertise to execute, such as electrical engineering design. Often includes the creation of original works (the transformation of knowledge to information).

2. *Transaction work.* Work requiring focus on the details of data input and management, such as transcription or account updates.

3. *Broker/coordinator work.* Work requiring interpersonal and communications skills with the ability to translate information from one level or worker group to another. Often includes the interpretation of information as opposed to the creation of original works.

4. *Integrated work.* Work that requires one to act or react to information but generally does not include the creation of original information.

IWPC. Information Work Productivity Council, a consortium of technology companies, academic leaders, and the business community organized in 2002 to research the concept of information work productivity.

Lean production. Concerned with getting the right things, to the right place, at the right time, in the right quantity while minimizing waste and being flexible and open to change.

Lean Six Sigma (LSS). A methodology to manage process variations that cause defects, defined as unacceptable deviation from the mean or target, and to systematically work toward managing variation to eliminate those defects.

Microsoft Office. Suite of software products including Microsoft Word, Excel, Access, PowerPoint, Outlook; may include additional products such as SharePoint and Visio.

Operational measures. Performance measures at a procedural (as opposed to a process) level.

Opportunity. A portion of the value stream (steps in a procedure) that is not performing at top effectiveness (quality) and/or efficiency (delivery or cycle speed).

Organizational capital. The procedures and practices that a firm implements in order to get the day's work done. If a factory or warehouse is the "hardware" of a firm, then organizational capital would be its software.

Performance lags. Issues or points in the procedure that cause a slowdown in production.

PCM. Productivity Capability Measures. The additional indicators of information flow, including indexes such as work and technology alignment.

PIF. Productivity Impact Framework. A summary-level name for the measurement program originally designed by Microsoft Consulting Services for the U.S. Air Force and other clients.

PIM. Productivity Impact Measures. A summary-level name for the measures provided by the Productivity Exchange (www.productivityexchange. org) to support productivity improvement programs.

POM. Productivity Opportunity Map. Mapping of the baseline state of a given work scenario.

Productivity. The amount of output created (in terms of goods produced or services rendered) per unit input used. For instance, labor productivity is typically measured as output per worker or output per labor-hour. With respect to land, the "yield" is equivalent to "land productivity." "Total factor productivity," sometimes called multifactor productivity, also includes both labor and capital goods in the denominator (weighted by their incomes).

Productivity challenge. Issues and production lags that cause a slowdown in worker productivity.

Process Cycle Efficiency (PCE). The percent of time within a procedure that is applied directly to the production of a customer identified deliverable. PCE does not include the time spent thinking or even communicating about the deliverable, just the time the customer would identify as going into the production of the deliverable.

Rework. The work step in which the defects found during review or inspection are resolved by the author, designer, or programmer.

Sarbanes–Oxley. Sarbanes–Oxley Act of 2002 (Pub. L. No. 107-204, 116 Stat. 745, also known as the Public Company Accounting Reform and Investor

Protection Act of 2002 and commonly called SOX). Wide-ranging legislation that establishes new or enhanced standards for all U.S. public companies, boards, management, and public accounting firms. The act contains 11 titles, or sections, ranging from additional corporate board responsibilities to criminal penalties, and requires the Securities and Exchange Commission to implement rulings on requirements to comply with the new law.

Taxonomy. A classification of things or the principles underlying the classification. Almost anything—animate objects, inanimate objects, places, and events—may be classified according to some taxonomic scheme. In terms of information work, it is the alignment of work to work behaviors.

Value stream. The steps within a procedure that are directly involved in the production of deliverables.

Work effectiveness. Consistent, leveraged, aligned, and relevant work.

Work efficiency. Cost-effective, speedy delivery.

Work scenario. The entire value stream, regardless of organizational alignment, required to deliver a specified set of objectives (deliverables). A work scenario is composed of a set of procedures and deliverables.

Work-tech alignment. The appropriate work behavior (activities) and technologies for a given work scenario.

Index